PRACTICAL ORCHESTRATION

PRACTICAL ORCHESTRATION

A Method of Arranging
for
School Orchestras

•

by
MERLE J. ISAAC

$8.00
In U.S.A.

ROBBINS MUSIC CORPORATION
1540 BROADWAY • NEW YORK 36, N. Y.

PRACTICAL ORCHESTRATION
A Method of Arranging for School Orchestras

This book is dedicated to all teachers and students of orchestration with the sincere hope that it will stimulate and encourage many to make contributions to the literature of the school orchestra.

ACKNOWLEDGMENTS

The author acknowledges with gratitude his indebtedness to many people for their assistance, encouragement, and stimulation:

Composers whose works exemplify the art of orchestration;

Authors whose books acquaint the orchestrator with the many and varied aspects of music;

Publishers who have made music and books available and who have kindly given permission to quote from their publications;

Directors and members of school orchestras who have demonstrated enthusiasm and musicianship when playing well-written compositions and arrangements;

Adele M. Ries whose editorial assistance with the manuscript was most helpful;

Arthur Tabachnick and Shirley Evans, professional musicians and teachers, whose suggestions and criticisms regarding writing for strings have been invaluable;

Joseph A. Levin, Editor-in-Chief, who gave freely of his time and talent in bridging the gap between manuscript and publication and who generously contributed the fourteenth chapter, "An Arranger Must Know About Copyright";

E. J. McCauley, Director of Educational Publications, who, with quiet devotion and deep sincerity, has done so much to promote music education in the schools of America;

And, finally, countless teachers, students, and co-workers who, in many varied ways through the years, have made innumerable contributions to a vast fund of knowledge that, to the orchestrator, is of immeasurable value.

INTRODUCTION

Orchestration is the art of arranging music so that it may be played by an orchestra. To write well, the arranger must possess (or acquire) many facts and skills, including the following:

1. A thorough knowledge of simple harmony and an understanding of the principles of voice leading;

2. A knowledge of instruments: their names, ranges, tone colors, and techniques;

3. A knowledge of what each instrument can do easily and effectively;

4. A knowledge of musical notation, including transposition;

5. The ability to play well on one member of each family of instruments (strings, woodwinds, brasses, and percussions), and at least a chromatic scale on all instruments;

6. Some facility at the piano keyboard.

Those who arrange music for school orchestras must also know something about the psychology of young people, how well they can be expected to read and play, and not only what music they like, but also what they can perform effectively, so that they will not be required to attempt music that demands greater maturity than they possess.

CONTENTS

CHAPTER ONE

THE STRINGS

The string family includes the violin, viola, cello, and bass. These are the most numerous and the most important instruments in the orchestra. They are, in fact, its foundation. The wind and percussion instruments add color, variety, volume, and rhythm.

To write well for the orchestra, one must write well for the strings. They are the most expressive and the most versatile of instruments, being able to produce music either slow and sustained or lively and rhythmic. String instruments can be played for long periods of time without tiring the players or becoming tiresome to the listeners.

The tones produced by the string family vary in pitch from very low to very high. All of the string instruments blend well with one another. Their dynamic range is great. Although a single string instrument cannot play very loudly, an entire string section can produce a resounding fortissimo. And no group of instruments can play more softly.

The instruments of the string family have a long history. For hundreds of years, in various parts of the world, people have played string instruments. Sometimes the instruments have had only one string; at other times they have had many.

The string instruments were perfected by Stradivarius and other great violin makers between 1600 A.D. and 1750 A.D. Since then, few changes have been made in their sizes and shapes. Many of the instruments made at that time are still in use.

String instruments are made almost entirely of wood. The violin and the viola are each constructed of about seventy pieces of various kinds of wood. The cello is quite similar, although there is some metal in the end pin that rests on the floor. The bass has metal machine pegs for tuning the strings. The kind and quality of the wood used in making any string instrument and the way that the wood is shaped and finished have much to do with the quality of the tone that can be produced on that instrument.

The strings used on instruments are made of gut, wire, or gut wound with wire. All four strings on an instrument are the same length, but they differ in weight and thickness. The thinner, lighter strings make high pitched sounds. The thicker, heavier strings make low pitched sounds. The lighter the string, the higher the pitch; the heavier the string, the lower the pitch.

The strings are fastened, at the lower end, to the tailpiece. At the upper end, each string is fastened to a separate, movable peg. A string is tuned by turning its peg which tightens or loosens it until it sounds the desired pitch. The tighter the string, the higher the pitch; the looser the string, the lower the pitch.

After a string is tuned, its pitch is changed by the player when he presses it down with the fingers of his left hand. When a string is bowed without being touched by the fingers, it vibrates its entire length from the bridge to the pegbox. When a finger is pressed on the string, it vibrates only from the bridge to the finger. As the player adds other fingers, or moves the finger closer to the bridge, the vibrating portion of the string becomes shorter. The longer the vibrating portion of the string, the lower the pitch; the shorter the vibrating portion, the higher the pitch.

For instance, when the first finger of the left hand is pressed down (in the right place) on the A string, the sound will be B. By pressing down the second finger on the same string, but a little closer to the bridge, the sound will be C. In the same way, the third and fourth fingers will sound D and E.

On all of the string instruments used in the orchestra, the characteristic tone is produced by means of a bow. This is a light, bent stick to which are fastened many strands of long horsehair that have been rubbed with rosin. When the hair is drawn across a tightened string, the string vibrates and makes a musical tone which is amplified by the hollow, wooden body of the instrument. For special effects, strings may be made to vibrate by plucking them. This method of producing the tone is known as *pizzicato*.

The bows used with the various string instruments are quite similar. The violin bow is the longest and the lightest. The viola bow is slightly heavier. The cello bow is shorter and heavier, and the bass bow is still shorter and heavier.

The bow is a very important part of a string instrument. It is largely the bow that brings out the beautiful, characteristic tone of a string instrument. The bow makes the tones loud or soft, connected or separated. Although the fingers of the player's left hand determine the pitch of the tones being played and the vibrato, the player's use of the right hand and arm in handling the bow determines, very largely, tone quality, volume, expression, rhythm, and style.

It might be possible to invent a machine to take the place of the left hand to finger the strings. It is doubtful, however, that a machine could be invented to take the place of the right hand and arm which control the bow.

THE VIOLIN

The violin is the soprano of the string family and the most important instrument in the orchestra. In the following example, the open notes indicate the four open strings of the violin, tuned in fifths. The closed notes indicate the tones obtained by placing the fingers on the strings.

Ex. 1

THE FIRST POSITION ON THE VIOLIN

Fingering: 0 1 2 3 4 0 1 2 3 4 0 1 2 3 4 0 1 2 3 4

Open strings: G   D   A   E

These tones, with their chromatic alterations, make up what the violinist calls the first position. Notice that three of the tones (D, A, and E) may be played either as open strings or with the fourth finger on the string next lower in pitch.

Higher tones, on each of the strings, may be obtained by moving the hand into higher positions (toward the bridge). For instance, on the A string, when the first finger plays B the hand is said to be in the first position. First finger playing C, second position; playing D, third position; playing E, fourth position; playing F, fifth position. Ex. 2 illustrates all of the tones (except the chromatic tones) that can be played in the first five positions of the violin on each of the four strings.

Ex. 2

THE FIRST FIVE POSITIONS ON THE VIOLIN

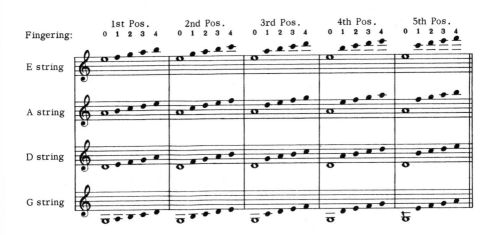

Music that has been written for school orchestras usually has a first violin part that is playable within the first five positions. Easy school music uses only the first position, or the first and third positions. As a rule, the second violin part is playable in the first position.

The quality of the tone produced with an open string is less pleasing than that obtained with a fingered (stopped) string. No vibrato is possible with an open string. Open strings should be avoided in slow passages, but may be used freely in rapid passages where they are less noticeable.

Because a player of a string instrument does not use his thumb on a string, only four fingers are numbered. Pianists should notice that fingers are numbered differently on string instruments.

Pianists should remember, also, that some skips which are difficult on the piano are not necessarily difficult on the violin. Ex. 3 illustrates skips which are easy and effective on the violin.

Ex. 3

a.

COURANTE

H. Eccles

b.

LINDA MUJER
(Guaracha)

Rafael Duchesne

© 1944 Robbins Music Corp.

Ex. 4 illustrates a two-octave interval which is quite a skip on the piano and on most other instruments. On the violin, this skip presents no fingering problem as the left hand does not move at all. There is, however, a bowing problem. The violin bow plays the low A on the G string, then crosses over to the E string for the high A.

Ex. 4

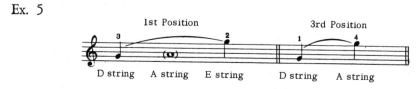

G string   E string

A violinist should not be required to skip back and forth from the lowest string to the highest because of the bowing problems. For example, he must stop the bow briefly as it crosses over the D string and the A string, and not let them sound. Slurring these wide-interval tones is really impossible, though a skillful player may fool the ear.

Ex. 5 illustrates a case where a violinist cannot slur two tones if he fingers them in the first position, for the open A string would be heard. By using the third position, however, the two tones can be played on adjacent strings, and they can be slurred easily.

Ex. 5

1st Position   3rd Position

D string   A string   E string   D string   A string

Chromatic tones on the violin are quite a different problem from chromatic tones on the piano and on most other instruments. For example, on the violin F♮ and F♯ on the D string are usually played with the same finger, but in slightly different places on the string. When these tones are played using the second finger, the violinist refers to the low second finger for F♮ and to the high second finger for F♯. The following illustration gives a typical fingering for a chromatic passage.

Ex. 6

FINGERING THE CHROMATIC SCALE ON THE VIOLIN

Passages with a large number of chromatic half-steps are not well suited to the violin, except for certain effects. In a chromatic passage, it is often necessary for a finger to slide a half-step from one tone to the next. Unless the bow stops between the tones or the violinist is quite skillful, the ear will hear the slide. To make each tone clear and distinct, a separate bow stroke is required for each tone, with a brief stop between the strokes. An occasional chromatic half-step in a slurred passage is not objectionable with capable players.

Ex. 7

DIMINISHED FIFTHS ON THE VIOLIN

The way in which chromatic tones are fingered on the violin presents another problem: diminished fifths. As seen in Ex. 7, F♮ and C♮ are played with the low second finger, and F♯ and C♯ are played with the high second finger. To play F♮ and C♮, together or in succession, it is possible to place the tip of the second finger on both of the strings at the same time, since the tones are exactly opposite each other on adjacent strings. The same is true of playing F♯ and C♯.

However, when playing C♮ and F♯ (a diminished fifth) in succession, the finger must be moved in two directions: across the finger-board from one string to another, and along the finger-board from the low position to the high position. This is not easy for the player to do, and these tones cannot be slurred satisfactorily without the use of special fingerings such as those illustrated in Ex. 8. This fingering device is similar to enharmonic notation: the F♯ is treated as though it were a G♭.

Ex. 8

DIMINISHED FIFTHS

Ex. 9

EASY DOUBLE-STOPS ON THE VIOLIN

On the violin, it is possible to play on two adjacent strings at the same time. This is known as playing double-stops. In (a) and (b) of Ex. 9, one of the two tones, in each case, is an open string. These double-stops are much easier to play than those at (c) and (d) where both tones must be fingered.

Double-stopping is an effective device for a violin solo, but it is of doubtful value when writing for a school orchestra. The tones will be played better in tune if they are played *divisi:* one player taking the lower note and another player taking the upper note. However, even this is not always effective with school orchestras which frequently have too few strings. Young players on strings do not get full volume from their instruments, and dividing a string section already lacking in volume further reduces its volume. Double-stopping and *divisi* playing should not be used, when writing for the string sections of school orchestras, except for special effects, such as playing softly a richly harmonized love song.

A standard symphony orchestra has thirty or more violin players divided into the first violin section and the second violin section. The instruments, of course, are the same, but the sections play different parts in the music. The first violins usually play the principal melodies in a composition, though they may play counter-melodies or accompaniment parts. The second violins may play some of the principal melodies with the first violins (in unison or in octaves), a duet with the first violins, or an accompaniment part.

A school orchestra with a small number of violin players may sound best when all of them play the first violin part. When there are enough violin players to provide adequate volume, an orchestra sounds very well with two violin sections playing two parts in duet style. Some kinds of music, such as popular waltz songs, sound especially effective when they are arranged in trio style. The third part may be played by the violas or by a third violin section which has the viola part written in the G clef.

Arrangements for school orchestras often have a part called "Advanced Violin." In this case, the first violin part is fairly easy, in the first position. The advanced part is much more difficult. Usually it has the same melodic line written an octave higher, requiring the use of the higher positions.

Ex. 10

VIOLIN

Violins may be used:

a. To play characteristic solo passages;

RUMANIAN OVERTURE

b. To play the principal melody, with or without other instruments;

(1)

OVER THE RAINBOW

E. Y. Harburg, Harold Arlen

Moderato

© 1939 Leo Feist Inc.

(2)

RUMANIAN OVERTURE

Merle J. Isaac

Allegro

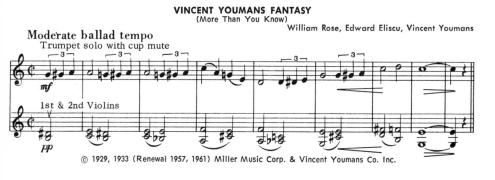

© 1954 Carl Fischer Inc.   Used by permission.

c. To play sustained accompaniment parts;

VINCENT YOUMANS FANTASY
(More Than You Know)

William Rose, Edward Eliscu, Vincent Youmans

Moderate ballad tempo
Trumpet solo with cup mute

1st & 2nd Violins

© 1929, 1933 (Renewal 1957, 1961) Miller Music Corp. & Vincent Youmans Co. Inc.

d. To play rhythmic accompaniment parts;

(1)

TEMPTATION

Arthur Freed, Nacio Herb Brown

Moderate beguine tempo
1st & 2nd Violins

Cellos

© 1933 (Renewal 1961) Metro-Goldwyn-Mayer Inc.   Copyright asgd. 1933 Robbins Music Corp. for U.S. & Canada

(2)

JEANNINE
(I Dream of Lilac Time)

L. Wolfe Gilbert, Nathaniel Shilkret

Valse moderato
1st & 2nd Violins-pizzicato

Cellos

© 1928 (Renewal 1956) Leo Feist Inc.

8

e. To play in duet style;

(1)

SANTA CLAUS IS COMIN' TO TOWN

Haven Gillespie, J. Fred Coots

Moderato
1st & 2nd Violins

© 1934 (Renewal 1962) Leo Feist Inc.

(2)

SONG OF LOVE from "Blossom Time"

Dorothy Donnelly, Sigmund Romberg

Tempo di valse
1st & 2nd Violins

© 1921 Karczag Pub Co. Inc.   Copyright Renewal 1949 Leo Feist Inc.

f. To play figuration;

MISSISSIPPI SUITE
(Mardi Gras)

Ferde Grofe

Maestoso e appassionato
1st & 2nd Violins

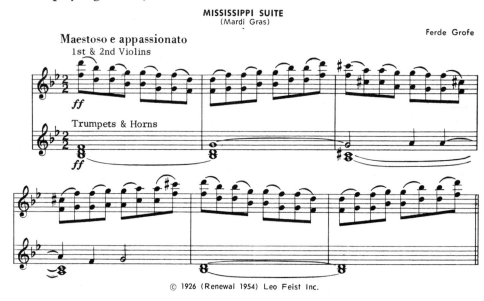

Trumpets & Horns

© 1926 (Renewal 1954) Leo Feist Inc.

THE VIOLA

The viola is the alto of the string family, but it can play tenor parts as well. It is slightly larger than the violin, although from a distance the two look very much alike.

Like the violin, the strings of the viola are tuned in fifths. The upper three strings of the viola (G, D, and A) are exactly the same in pitch as the lower three strings on the violin. The violin has a high E string, while the viola has a low C string.

Ex. 11

OPEN STRINGS

Violin   Viola

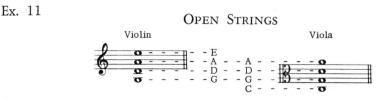

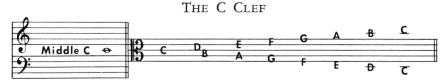

9

Music for the viola is written in the C clef. This clef, as used for the viola, designates the middle line of the staff as middle C. (Memorize: *middle line is middle C*).

Ex. 12

THE C CLEF

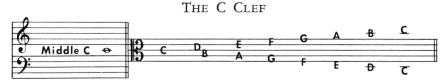

At first the arranger may find that learning the C clef is a problem. Its use, however, eliminates the great number of leger lines that would be required were either the G clef or the F clef used for viola music.

Ex. 13

a. Written with the G clef.

b. The same tones with the C clef.

c. Written with the F clef.

d. The same tones with the C clef.

In the following illustration, the open notes indicate the four open strings of the viola, tuned in fifths. The closed notes indicate the tones obtained by placing the fingers on the strings.

These tones, with their chromatic alterations, make up what the violist calls the first position. Notice that three of the tones (G, D, and A) may be played either as open strings or with the fourth finger on the string next lower in pitch.

Ex. 14

THE FIRST POSITION ON THE VIOLA

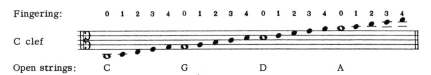

Ex. 15 illustrates the same notes as those shown in Ex. 14, using F clef and G clef notation.

Ex. 15

Higher tones, on all of the strings, may be obtained by moving the hand into higher positions. Ex. 16 illustrates all of the non-chromatic tones that can be obtained on all of the strings in the first three positions.

Ex. 16

THE FIRST THREE POSITIONS ON THE VIOLA

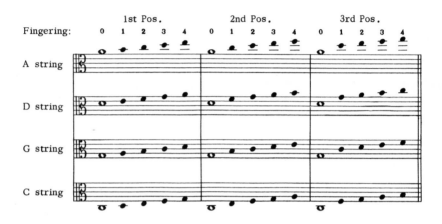

Viola parts, arranged for school orchestras, are usually written in the first position. Almost everything that applies to violin playing applies to viola playing as well. The problems of skips, chromatics, diminished fifths, and double-stops are essentially the same on both instruments. For a discussion of these problems see the section on the violin.

The violas need not have the principal melody to play, but should have a melodic part whenever possible. Viola players do not like to play after-beat accompaniments any better than the first violin players like to play them. A musical part is more likely to be played in a musical manner. Since the viola sections of most school orchestras are lacking in numbers and ability, it is especially necessary for the arranger to write a viola part that is playable and interesting.

The three parts for the first and second violins and the violas should be written so that the violins sound satisfactory without the violas, but much better with them. Play the following example (on strings or piano), noticing that the two violin parts are satisfactory without the viola part, but much more complete with it.

Ex. 17

A standard symphony orchestra has ten or twelve viola players. Although the violas usually play an alto or a tenor part, sometimes they play one of the principal melodies (often with another instrument) or a rhythmic accompaniment part.

Ex. 18

VIOLA

Violas may be used:

a. To play characteristic solo passages;

LULLABY

W. A. Mozart
Arr. Merle J. Isaac

© 1942 Remick Music Corp.   Used by permission.

b. To play the principal melody with other instruments (in unison or octaves);

(1)   **TEMPTATION**

Arthur Freed, Nacio Herb Brown

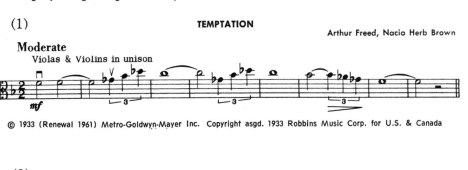

© 1933 (Renewal 1961) Metro-Goldwyn-Mayer Inc. Copyright asgd. 1933 Robbins Music Corp. for U.S. & Canada

(2)   **MISSISSIPPI SUITE**
(Mardi Gras)

Ferde Grofe

© 1926 (Renewal 1954) Leo Feist Inc.

c. To play sustained accompaniment parts;

VINCENT YOUMANS FANTASY
(More Than You Know)

William Rose, Edward Eliscu, Vincent Youmans

© 1929, 1933 (Renewal 1957, 1961) Miller Music Corp. & Vincent Youmans Co. Inc.

12

d. To play rhythmic accompaniment parts;

(1)   RENDEZVOUS

W. Aletter
Arr. Merle J. Isaac

(2)   MEXICAN OVERTURE

Merle J. Isaac

e. To play figurations;

MISSISSIPPI SUITE
(Mardi Gras)

Ferde Grofe

Ex. 19

VIOLINS AND VIOLAS

Some of the ways of combining the first violins, second violins, and violas are shown in the following illustrations:

a. First violins: melody; second violins and violas: after-beats.

(1)   BLUE MOON

Lorenz Hart, Richard Rodgers

(2)

CSARDAS

V. Monti
Arr. Merle J. Isaac

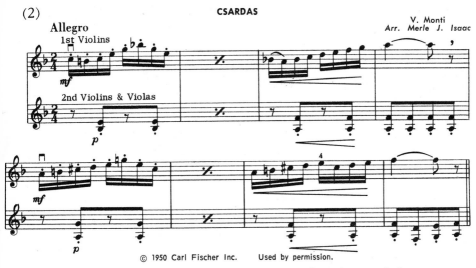

© 1950 Carl Fischer Inc.   Used by permission.

b. First violins: counter-melody; second violins and violas: melody.

RUSSIAN SAILORS' DANCE
from "The Red Poppy"

Reinhold Glière
Arr. Merle J. Isaac

© 1940 Carl Fischer Inc.   Used by permission.

c. Two violins and viola in trio style.

(1)

IN A LITTLE SPANISH TOWN
('Twas On A Night Like This)

Lewis & Young, Mabel Wayne

© 1926 (Renewal 1954) Leo Feist Inc.

(2)

OYE NEGRA
(Guaracha)

Noro Morales

Tempo di guaracha
1st & 2nd Violins

d. Three distinctly different parts.

BLOSSOM TIME SELECTION
(My Springtime Thou Art)

Dorothy Donnelly, Sigmund Romberg

Moderato
1st Violins

THE CELLO
(Violoncello)

The cello is the tenor of the string family, but it can play bass parts effectively, too. In the following illustration, the open notes indicate the four open strings of the cello, tuned in fifths. The closed notes indicate the tones obtained by placing the fingers on the strings in the usual way.

Ex. 20

THE FIRST POSITION ON THE CELLO

Fingering: 0 1 2 3 4 0 1 2 3 4 0 1 2 3 4 0 1 2 3 4

Open strings: C   G   D   A

Fingering on the cello is more difficult than fingering on the violin or viola. While the open strings of the cello are exactly one octave below the open strings of the viola (and have the same names), the cello's longer strings require a different system of fingering.

Notice that F♮ and F♯ (on the D string) are *not* played with the same finger on the cello as they are on the violin and viola.

Ex. 21

Notice that, unlike the violin and viola, the fourth finger tone on the cello (in the first position) is *not* the same as the next open string.

Ex. 22

THE FOURTH FINGER

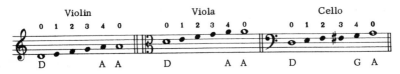

Where the violinist has the interval of a fourth under his fingers in any one position, the cellist has only a third. Normally, the cellist plays a minor third with his first and fourth fingers. By using an extended hand position, however, he may play a major third.

Ex. 23

EXTENSIONS

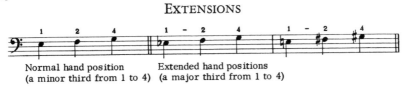

Normal hand position   Extended hand positions
(a minor third from 1 to 4)   (a major third from 1 to 4)

The use of an extension in cello fingering may be indicated by a dash, as shown above. A cellist would say that the dash means "stretch".

Ex. 24 illustrates all of the tones that can be played on the cello in the first four positions without using extended hand positions.

Ex. 24

THE FIRST FOUR POSITIONS ON THE CELLO

Cello parts, written for school orchestras, need not be limited to the use of the first position. In fact, a cello part written entirely in the first position may actually be more difficult to play than one which uses the higher positions.

A cello part will not necessarily be difficult if it requires the use of the first four positions on the two upper strings, as cello students study these fingering problems rather early in their training. To be playable and effective, a part should not require a cellist to shift positions too frequently. He should be able to remain in one position for several notes before shifting to another position for another group of notes. Good writing for the cello requires thoughtful planning.

Although the principal melody is not given to the cello section very often, the cello part is usually melodic, particularly when it is tenor in character, rather than bass. Sustained counter-melodies played in the upper register of the cello are warm, intense, and beautiful.

It is possible to play double-stops and chords on the cello, but they should be used rarely when writing for school orchestras. They are likely to be played out of tune, and so will weaken the harmony rather than strengthen it. Illustrated below are a few easy and effective chords, using one or two open strings, which may be used sparingly.

Ex. 25

CHORDS

Some broken chords or arpeggios are quite playable and useful, slurred or detached. Notice that the ones illustrated contain one or more open strings.

Ex. 26

ARPEGGIOS

A symphony orchestra usually has ten cello players. The cellos may play one of the principal melodies or they may play a bass part. They are especially beautiful, however, when playing a counter-melody.

Ex. 27

CELLO

Cellos may be used:

a. To play characteristic solo passages;

SYMPHONY No. 8
(The "Unfinished")

Franz Schubert

b. To play melodies with other instruments (in unison or in octaves);

(1) **TEMPTATION**

Arthur Freed, Nacio Herb Brown

Moderate beguine tempo
Cellos & Violins in octaves

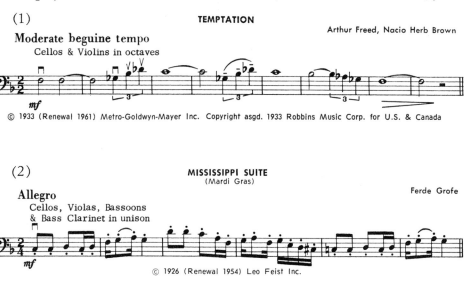

© 1933 (Renewal 1961) Metro-Goldwyn-Mayer Inc. Copyright asgd. 1933 Robbins Music Corp. for U.S. & Canada

(2) **MISSISSIPPI SUITE**
(Mardi Gras)

Ferde Grofe

Allegro
Cellos, Violas, Bassoons
& Bass Clarinet in unison

© 1926 (Renewal 1954) Leo Feist Inc.

c. To play counter-melodies;

SONG OF LOVE from "Blossom Time"

Dorothy Donnelly, Sigmund Romberg

Moderately
Violins & Violas

Cellos

© 1921 Karczag Pub Co. Inc.   Copyright Renewal 1949 Leo Feist Inc.

d. To play sustained bass parts;

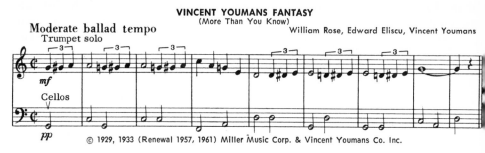

VINCENT YOUMANS FANTASY
(More Than You Know)

Moderate ballad tempo

William Rose, Edward Eliscu, Vincent Youmans

Trumpet solo

e. To play rhythmic bass parts;

SIBONEY

Ernesto Lecuona, Dolly Morse

Tempo di rhumba

1st Violins

f. To play broken chords or arpeggios;

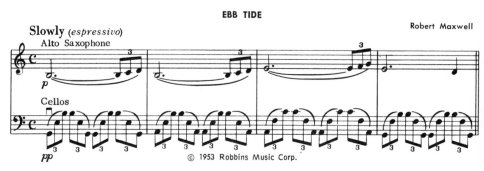

EBB TIDE

Robert Maxwell

Slowly (*espressivo*)

Alto Saxophone

THE BASS

The bass, of course, is the bass of the string family. It is also known as a string bass, a double bass, or a bass viol, but *not* as a bass violin.

Music for the bass is written in the F clef, but the tones sound an octave lower than they are written. This method of notation is used to avoid the use of many leger lines below the staff.

Ex. 28

WRITTEN   SOUNDS

In the following illustration, the open notes indicate the four open strings of the bass, tuned in fourths. (The names of the open strings on the bass are the same as those on the violin, but in reverse order!) The closed notes indicate the tones obtained by placing the fingers on the strings in the first position.

Ex. 29

THE FIRST POSITION ON THE BASS

Because of its very large size, the bass uses a system of fingering that is quite different from that used by the other string instruments. Since the strings are longer, the tones are farther apart. On a violin or a viola, the harmonic interval between the first and fourth fingers is a fourth; on a cello, a third; on a bass, a second (just one whole-step!). See Ex. 30.

Ex. 30

On the bass, the fingering 1-4 is used for whole-steps and either 1-2 or 2-4 for half-steps. The third finger is not used at all, except in the very high positions. Fingers are not shifted for chromatic tones, as on a violin.

The bass differs, too, in that it has half-positions between several of the positions. In the following illustration, the open notes indicate the four open strings of the bass, tuned in fourths. The closed notes indicate the tones obtained by placing the fingers on the strings.

Ex. 31

THE LOWER POSITIONS ON THE BASS

A good bass part is melodic and singable, although not like a soprano part. A bass part usually contains more skips than a soprano melody would be likely to have, but it should also have a number of scale-wise steps. Most bass passages contain notes that are in two or more positions, and frequent shifting is required.

Although rapid passages can be played on the bass they are not very effective as they cannot be heard clearly.

The low E string is not sufficiently clear and well-defined in pitch for the average ear. It is best to have most of the bass part playable on the three upper strings.

A symphony orchestra has eight or ten players in the bass section. This important group provides the foundation for the melodies and harmonies in the music. If the bass section in a school orchestra plays well in tune, the entire orchestra plays better in tune.

Ex. 32

BASS

Basses may be used:

a. To play characteristic solo passages;

b. To play melodies with other instruments (in unison or in octaves);

c. To play sustained bass parts;

d. To play rhythmic bass parts;

(1)

MARCHING ALONG TOGETHER

Edward Pola, Franz Steininger

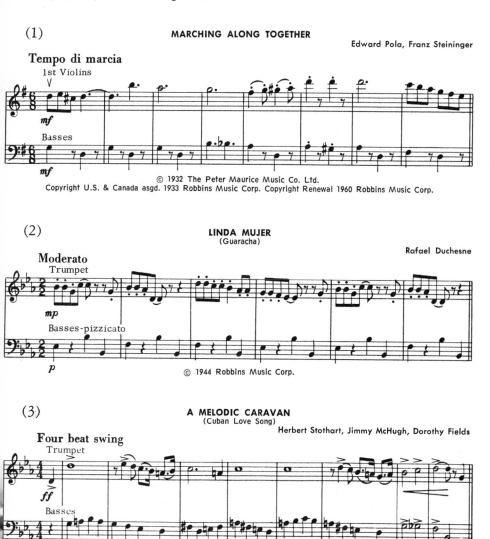

© 1932 The Peter Maurice Music Co. Ltd.
Copyright U.S. & Canada asgd. 1933 Robbins Music Corp. Copyright Renewal 1960 Robbins Music Corp.

(2)

LINDA MUJER
(Guaracha)

Rafael Duchesne

© 1944 Robbins Music Corp.

(3.)

A MELODIC CARAVAN
(Cuban Love Song)
Herbert Stothart, Jimmy McHugh, Dorothy Fields

© 1931 (Renewal 1959) Metro-Goldwyn-Mayer Inc.

CHAPTER TWO

THE WOODWINDS

While all of the string instruments resemble one another in tone color, the woodwind instruments differ greatly. A violin and a cello sound very much alike (except as to pitch), but a flute and a bassoon sound quite different.

Composers and arrangers enjoy writing for the various members of the woodwind family. By themselves, the woodwinds make a lovely choir. Used individually or in various combinations, the woodwind instruments add many beautiful and different tone colors to the music.

The woodwind family includes four groups of instruments:

Flute Group	*Oboe Group*	*Clarinet Group*	*Saxophone Group*
Flute	Oboe	B♭ Clarinet	E♭ Alto Saxophone
Piccolo	Bassoon	B♭ Bass Clarinet	B♭ Tenor Saxophone

A woodwind instrument consists of a tube, with a series of holes in the side, and a mouthpiece, with a reed, at one end. The player blows into the mouthpiece, causing the reed to vibrate. This, in turn, causes the air column within the instrument to vibrate, making a musical tone.

The flute group does not use a real reed, but the stream of air that the player directs across and into the mouthpiece serves as a reed, and causes the air column within the instrument to vibrate.

The oboe group uses a double reed, made of cane, that looks very much like a soda straw flattened at one end.

The clarinet and saxophone groups use a single reed (a flat piece of cane, very thin at one end) which fastens to a chisel-shaped mouthpiece.

Some of the finger-holes on woodwind instruments are covered by the player's finger-tips. Others are covered by padded keys which are controlled by the player's fingers. When all of the holes are covered, the player can set into vibration the entire length of the air column within the instrument.

As the fingers are lifted, starting at the lower end of the instrument, the holes are opened, the vibrating air column becomes shorter, and the pitch of the tone becomes higher. The shorter the vibrating air column, the higher the pitch. The longer the vibrating air column, the lower the pitch.

Ex. 33

FINGERING PLAN FOR WOODWIND INSTRUMENTS

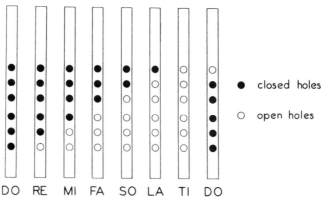

● closed holes

○ open holes

DO RE MI FA SO LA TI DO

This method of changing the pitch of a tone on a woodwind instrument may be used for one octave (a twelfth on the clarinets).

There are different ways of obtaining a second (higher) octave on the various woodwind instruments:

1. by blowing somewhat differently;
2. by using a slightly different fingering;
3. by using an octave or register key.

The third octave (very high in pitch) requires fingerings that are quite different.

Chromatic tones are obtained on woodwind instruments by the use of keys which open or close holes located between the regular finger-holes. Chromatic scales and passages are not difficult on woodwind instruments and may be very effective.

While players of string instruments can play for long periods of time without tiring, players of wind instruments must rest from time to time, partly for breathing and partly to give their embouchure muscles an opportunity to relax.

The listeners, too, appreciate the wind instruments more if they do not play continuously.

THE FLUTE

The flute is probably the oldest wind instrument known. Flutes were used by the ancient Egyptians five thousand years ago.

Around 1830, a German flutist named Theobald Boehm (Baym) invented a new system of keys for the flute. This system simplified the fingering and made it easier to play the instrument in tune.

The modern flute is usually made of metal, and it is about 26½ inches long. The tone is made by blowing across and into the hole in the side of the mouthpiece. This is much like blowing gently across and into the mouth of a bottle.

Music for the flute is usually written within the range shown below, and it sounds as written. The closed notes indicate the effective range for school orchestras.

Ex. 34

FLUTE

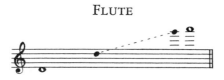

While the flute can play down to middle C, the low register is of little value in writing for school orchestras. The low register is very beautiful, but it is so soft that the rest of the orchestra would almost have to stop playing to let the flutes be heard.

From about D on the fourth line to the high G, the flute tone is clear and bright. This is the most useful and effective register of the instrument.

Music for the flute usually requires the use of many leger lines above the staff. Flute players are accustomed to music which is written this way, and they do not find it difficult to read. They do not like to have the part written on the staff and marked *8va* or "Play an octave higher", devices popular with pianists.

Most music arranged for school orchestras has two flute parts, marked "first flute" and "second flute". The second flute part is usually easier to play than the first flute part, and it is lower in pitch. It is customary for the second flute player to double on piccolo when the music calls for this instrument. If the piccolo part is important and difficult, however, it would be played better by the first flute player.

A large orchestra may have four flute players, with two on the first part and two on the second part. If the composer wishes a passage to be played by one player only, the passage is marked "Solo". Music for symphony orchestras may have three flute parts, while easy music for school use may have only one flute part.

THE PICCOLO

The piccolo is a small flute, usually made of metal, about 12½ inches long (nearly half the length of the flute, though it seems much smaller). The piccolo plays an octave higher than the flute.

The tone is made by blowing a small stream of air across and into the mouthpiece, the same as on the flute. The piccolo requires the same fingerings as the flute. Since the instruments are so similar, flute players often double on piccolo.

Music for the piccolo is usually written within the range shown below, but it sounds an octave higher. The closed notes indicate the effective range for school orchestras.

Ex. 35

PICCOLO

The lower tones of the piccolo cannot be played loudly, and the upper tones cannot be played softly. The piccolo is a very lively instrument, the most agile of the wind instruments. It can play rapid passages brilliantly, and it adds sparkle and ornamentation to the music. It is not effective in long sustained tones.

Most music written for school orchestras does not require a piccolo. When one is called for, it is generally used when the full orchestra is playing *forte,* or for special descriptive effects.

Ex. 36

FLUTE

Flutes may be used:

a. To play characteristic solo passages;

MORNING MOOD
from Peer Gynt, Suite No. 1

Edvard Grieg

b. To play the principal melody with other instruments, in unison or in octaves;

(1)

MISSISSIPPI SUITE
(Mardi Gras)

Ferde Grofe

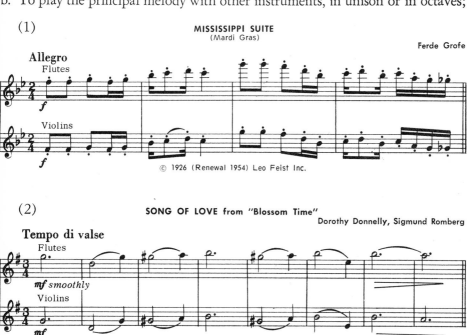

© 1926 (Renewal 1954) Leo Feist Inc.

(2)

SONG OF LOVE from "Blossom Time"
Dorothy Donnelly, Sigmund Romberg

© 1921 Karczag Pub Co. Inc.   Copyright Renewal 1949 Leo Feist Inc.

c. To play passages with ornamental figuration;

OVER THE RAINBOW

E. Y. Harburg, Harold Arlen

© 1939 Leo Feist Inc.

d. To play obbligatos and counter-melodies;

MEXICAN OVERTURE

Merle J. Isaac

e. To play long trills;

OUR DIRECTOR

F. E. Bigelow
Arr. Merle J. Isaac

THE OBOE

The oboe is another soprano voice in the woodwind family. It is a wooden instrument about 23 inches long and, from a distance, it looks very much like a clarinet. The oboe, however, is a double reed instrument, and its mouthpiece differs greatly from that of the clarinet.

Music for the oboe is usually written within the range shown below, and it sounds as written. The closed notes indicate the practical school range.

Ex. 37

OBOE

Its tone quality, somewhat reedy and nasal, enables the oboe to be heard clearly, even in a large orchestra. In fact, the oboe tone is so penetrating that the arranger must be careful to write the oboe part with this in mind, and not give it a subordinate part, one that should not be too prominent. On the oboe, it is difficult to play softly the lowest and the highest tones. While it can play fairly rapid passages, the oboe is at its best playing song-like melodies, happy or sad, but always sweet.

A symphony orchestra has two oboes and an English horn. The latter is an alto oboe in F.

Oboe players often double on the English horn as the two instruments are quite similar. Because few schools have an English horn (although it is a beautiful instrument and fairly easy to play) the instrument will not be considered in this book.

School orchestra music is written with either one oboe part or two. When there are two parts, the second is lower in pitch than the first and easier to play. The arranger must be careful not to let the second oboe part go too low as this register tends to be loud and somewhat rough.

Ex. 38

OBOE

Oboes may be used:

1. To play characteristic solo passages;

LEGEND
(Tone Poem)

Merle J. Isaac

Moderato

© 1941 Carl Fischer Inc.   Used by permission.

2. To play the principal melody with other instruments, in unison or in octaves;

MISSISSIPPI SUITE
(Mardi Gras)

Ferde Grofe

Andantino
Flute, Oboe, Trumpet, and Violin in octaves

© 1926 (Renewal 1954) Leo Feist Inc.

3. To play in duet form with other woodwind instruments;

RUMANIAN OVERTURE

Merle J. Isaac

Allegro
Flute

Oboe

© 1954 Carl Fischer Inc.   Used by permission.

28

d. To play counter-melodies;

A MELODIC CARAVAN
(It's A Most Unusual Day)

Harold Adamson, Jimmy McHugh

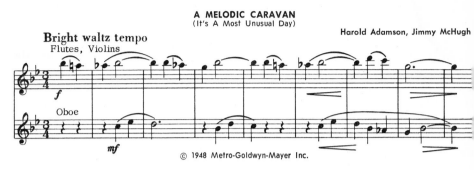

© 1948 Metro-Goldwyn-Mayer Inc.

e. To play sustained tones as background harmony;

VINCENT YOUMANS FANTASY
(Great Day)

Edward Eliscu, William Rose, Vincent Youmans

© 1929 (Renewal 1957) Miller Music Corp. & Vincent Youmans Co. Inc.

f. To play ornamental figures with other woodwind instruments;

A MELODIC CARAVAN
(I Feel A Song Comin' On)

Jimmy McHugh, Dorothy Fields, George Oppenheimer

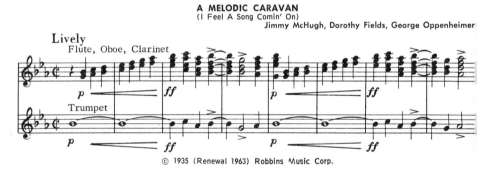

© 1935 (Renewal 1963) Robbins Music Corp.

g. To play rhythmic figures with muted trumpets;

THE GREAT DIVIDE

Louis Maurice

© 1907 (Renewal 1935) Leo Feist Inc.

THE BASSOON

The bassoon is the bass of the double-reed group and, traditionally, the bass of the orchestral woodwinds.

The bassoon is a wooden instrument about 8 feet long, shaped somewhat like the letter U. It is more difficult to finger than the other members of the woodwind family. This is partly because it is larger and the finger-holes are farther apart, and partly because it lacks the perfected mechanism of the modern flute, oboe, or clarinet.

Music for the bassoon is usually written within the range shown below, and it sounds as written. The closed notes indicate the practical school range.

Ex. 39

BASSOON

Although the bassoon and the oboe are both double-reed instruments, they differ in many ways. The tone of the oboe is reedy and penetrating, and unless it is played skillfully it does not blend with the other instruments. The tone of the bassoon, however, is reedy only in its lowest register. The other registers blend very well with the other instruments. In fact, in some ways, the bassoon tone blends too well. For example, when bassoons are playing in unison or in octaves with the string basses, the bassoon tone will not be heard as such. The string bass tone, however, will have a clarity of line that it would not have otherwise. Two bassoons and two horns, playing four-part harmony, sound much like four horns. The bassoon tone is absorbed by the tones of the other instruments to their benefit.

The upper register of the bassoon is weak in volume, being much softer than clarinet tones of the same pitch. Most bassoon parts written for school orchestras make little use of the high register, and most school bassoon players are not familiar with it.

The bassoon can play a solo part most effectively, though it needs a suitable accompaniment to enable it to be heard (except in the lowest register). However, the bassoon is most useful when it is reinforcing other bass and tenor instruments.

A symphony orchestra has from two to four bassoon players, one of whom may double on the contra-bassoon. (The contra-bassoon is so rarely found in school orchestras that it is not discussed in this book.) School orchestras seldom have more than two bassoon players, and one part played by both may sound better than two separate parts.

Ex. 40

BASSOON

Bassoons may be used:

a. To play characteristic solo passages;

MISSISSIPPI SUITE
(Huckleberry Finn)

Ferde Grofe

Scherzando

© 1926 (Renewal 1954) Leo Feist Inc.

b. To double the principal melody with other instruments, in unison or in octaves;

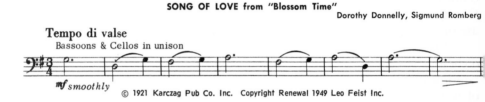

SONG OF LOVE from "Blossom Time"
Dorothy Donnelly, Sigmund Romberg

Tempo di valse
Bassoons & Cellos in unison

© 1921 Karczag Pub Co. Inc. Copyright Renewal 1949 Leo Feist Inc.

c. To play a bass part;

LINDA MUJER
(Guaracha)

Rafael Duchesne

Moderato

© 1944 Robbins Music Corp.

d. To play sustained tones as background harmony;

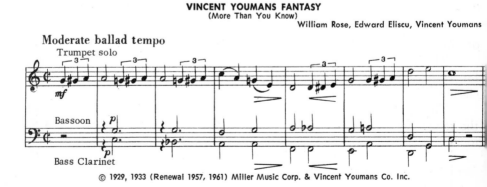

VINCENT YOUMANS FANTASY
(More Than You Know)

William Rose, Edward Eliscu, Vincent Youmans

Moderate ballad tempo
Trumpet solo

Bassoon

Bass Clarinet

© 1929, 1933 (Renewal 1957, 1961) Miller Music Corp. & Vincent Youmans Co. Inc.

e. To play counter-melodies;

RUMANIAN OVERTURE

Merle J. Isaac

THE Bb CLARINET

While primitive single reed instruments have been known for many centuries, it is believed that the clarinet was invented by Johann Denner in Germany about 1690. The instrument was greatly improved in 1843 by the use of the Boehm system of construction and fingering.

Clarinets are made in several sizes, but the only one used in school orchestras is the Bb clarinet. (The bass clarinet will be considered as a separate instrument.) The Bb clarinet is about 26 inches long, and may be made of wood, metal, ebonite, or plastic.

The clarinet is the most useful member of the woodwind family. Its tone is generally very pleasing, blending well with all other instruments.

Music for the Bb clarinet is usually written within the range shown below, but it sounds one whole-step (a major second) lower.* The closed notes indicate the practical school range.

Ex. 41

Bb CLARINET

WRITTEN   SOUNDS

The clarinet has a range of nearly three octaves and may be played fast or slow, loud or soft.

The low register, which is a rich alto voice, is very useful and very beautiful. Unlike some of the other woodwind instruments, the low register of the clarinet is neither too soft nor too loud. It may be used freely.

The upper register, a clear soprano voice, may also be used freely within the range given in the examples. It is possible to play much higher, but the tones are less satisfactory for orchestral use.

*For an explanation of the transposing instruments, see the chapter on transposition.

The Clarinet Registers*

lower register   weak register   upper register

As shown in Ex. 42, there are a few weak tones in the middle register which require some attention from the arranger. These tones should not be used for sustained melodic passages, as it is not easy to play them in tune with good tone quality.

These tones also present a problem in fingering. When the clarinetist plays G♯ (concert), he has almost all of his fingers raised. In order to play A, he must put all of his fingers down very quickly on many different keys. It is not easy to go from G♯ to A and back again.

Most woodwind instruments overblow an octave. That is, the fingering for G in the lower register is about the same as that for G an octave higher. The clarinet, however, overblows a twelfth. The fingering for G in the lower register, with the addition of the register key, will produce D, a twelfth higher. In the example given below, the notes at (a) and those at (b) are fingered in the same way, except that the register key is opened for the second group.

Ex. 43

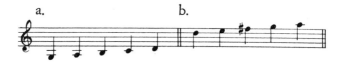

a.   b.

While not as agile as the flute, the clarinet can play rapid scales, arpeggios, and trills. It has great dynamic range, and can be played with much expression.

Music arranged for school orchestras has two B♭ clarinet parts, a first and a second. The second part, lower in pitch than the first, is usually easier to play. If the composer wishes a passage to be played by only one player, the passage is marked "Solo". In a symphony orchestra, one of the clarinet players doubles on the bass clarinet. We do not ask this of school orchestra clarinetists.

Textbooks on orchestration always discuss the A clarinet, and usually advise its use when the orchestra is playing in certain keys: those having several sharps in the signature. However, school orchestra players seldom have A clarinets, and professional players usually play the A clarinet parts on the B♭ clarinet by transposing as they play. Except in very special cases, it is not necessary to write for the A clarinet, and even then it is well to include a transposed part for the B♭ clarinet in case no A clarinet is available.

*The notation in Ex. 42 indicates the tones actually sounded by the B♭ clarinet. They are written one whole-step higher.

The A clarinet is a little longer than the B♭ clarinet, and it sounds a minor third lower than the written notes.

Ex. 44

Ex. 45

B♭ CLARINET

(All of the following examples, except (a), are shown as they sound, not as they are written.)

Clarinets may be used:

a. To play characteristic solo passages;

CAPRICCIO ESPAGNOL

N. Rimsky-Korsakov

b. To play the principal melody with other instruments, in unison or in octaves;

(1)

TEMPTATION

Arthur Freed, Nacio Herb Brown

(2)

OUR DIRECTOR

F. E. Bigelow
Arr. Merle J. Isaac

34

c. To play in duet form, with another clarinet or with another instrument;

RAMONA

L. Wolfe Gilbert, Mabel Wayne

d. To play counter-melodies;

MY OWN AMERICA

Allie Wrubel

e. To play sustained tones as background harmony;

PAGAN LOVE SONG

Arthur Freed, Nacio Herb Brown

f. To play ornamental figures with other woodwind instruments;

(1)

GYPSY LIFE
from "The Fortune Teller"

Victor Herbert
Arr. Merle J. Isaac

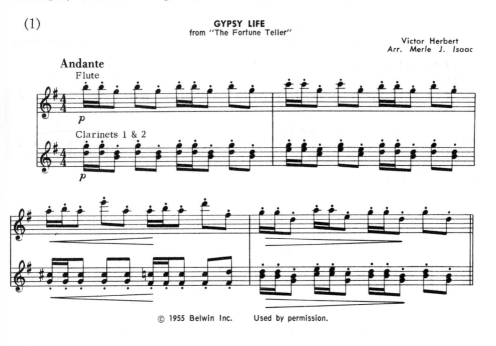

(2)

SONG OF LOVE from "Blossom Time"
Dorothy Donnelly, Sigmund Romberg

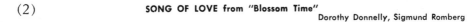

g. To play long trills;

MISSISSIPPI SUITE
(Father Of Waters)

Ferde Grofe

THE BASS CLARINET

The B♭ bass clarinet is about 4½ feet long. The body of the instrument may be made of wood, metal, ebonite, or plastic. At the upper end is a large bent metal tube, and the lower end is a large metal bell, much like that of a saxophone.

The bass clarinet provides a beautiful bass for passages played by the woodwind family. Its rich tone blends well with that of other instruments. It is especially beautiful when playing sustained passages very softly.

Music for the B♭ bass clarinet is usually written within the range shown below, but it sounds a major ninth lower. The closed notes indicate the practical school range.

Ex. 46

Bass Clarinet

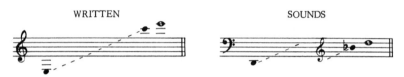

The bass clarinet uses the same fingering as the B♭ clarinet and is similar in many other ways. It has the same weak middle register. The lower register is the most useful for orchestra playing.

Ex. 47

The Registers of the Bass Clarinet

This notation indicates the tones actually sounded by the B♭ bass clarinet. They are written a major ninth higher.

In symphony orchestras, the second or third clarinet player often doubles on bass clarinet. In school orchestras, however, clarinet players are not expected to double.

The schools of America own many bass clarinets, and there are many capable players using these instruments. Although the instruments and the players are usually associated with school bands, rather than with school orchestras, this need not be so.

Traditionally, the bassoon is the bass of the orchestral woodwinds, and the bass clarinet is used for special effects only. However, in the schools there are more bass clarinet players and instruments available than bassoon players and instruments. The bass clarinet blends well with other instruments and ably assists bassoon and string bass sections which, in school orchestras, are usually weak.

There is no musical or educational reason why the bass clarinet should not be accepted as a regular member of the school orchestra.

Ex. 48

Bass Clarinet

(In the following examples, the bass clarinet part is given as it sounds, not as it is written.)

Bass Clarinets may be used:

a. To play characteristic solo passages;

THE NUTCRACKER SUITE

P. I. Tchaikovsky

Andante non troppo

b. To play a melody with other instruments;

MISSISSIPPI SUITE
(Mardi Gras)

Ferde Grofe

Allegro

© 1926 (Renewal 1954) Leo Feist Inc.

c. To play a sustained bass part;

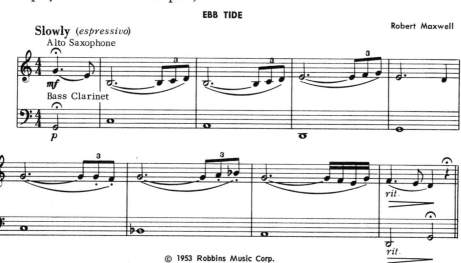

EBB TIDE

Robert Maxwell

Slowly (*espressivo*)

© 1953 Robbins Music Corp.

d. To play a rhythmic bass part;

(1)

SANTA CLAUS IS COMIN' TO TOWN

Haven Gillespie, J. Fred Coots

© 1934 (Renewal 1962) Leo Feist Inc.

(2)

OYE NEGRA
(Guaracha)

Noro Morales

© 1942 Robbins Music Corp.

THE SAXOPHONES

The invention of the saxophone by Antoine Sax in 1840 was an accident. Sax put a clarinet mouthpiece on a brass horn and found that he had invented a new instrument. It sounded neither like a clarinet nor like a horn.

Although the saxophone is made of brass, it is usually grouped with the woodwind family. Its tone is produced with a single reed and mouthpiece similar to a clarinet reed and mouthpiece. Saxophones finger very much like oboes and flutes.

The saxophone group includes a whole family of instruments varying in size from the small soprano saxophone to the large bass saxophone. If a school orchestra uses saxophones, they will be either altos or tenors or both.

Music for all of the saxophones is usually written within the range given below, but sounds lower:

The Eb alto saxophone sounds a major sixth lower;

The Bb tenor saxophone sounds a major ninth lower.

The arranger, therefore, must write saxophone parts correspondingly higher.

Ex. 49

SAXOPHONES

The practical school orchestra range for the saxophones omits the top and bottom tones because of their tone quality, rather than because of their difficulty.

Saxophones can play rapid scale-like passages with ease, but cannot play repeated tones rapidly.

Although they are essential instruments in concert bands and indispensable members of dance bands, saxophones are used rarely in symphony orchestras. The saxophone tone does not seem to blend well with those of the other orchestral instruments, possibly because the instrument is too often played in a style better suited to dance music.

Saxophones are used in school orchestras as optional instruments. They do not, as a rule, have an essential part of their own, but may substitute for horns, bassoons, or other instruments which may be missing. An exception to this practice would be an arrangement for school orchestra of a composition which in its original form included essential saxophone parts.

Published arrangements for school orchestra usually include an optional part for the E♭ alto saxophone and one for the B♭ tenor saxophone.

Ex. 50

SAXOPHONES

(All of the examples, except (a), show the saxophone tones as they actually sound, not as they are written.)

Saxophones may be used:

a. To play characteristic solos;

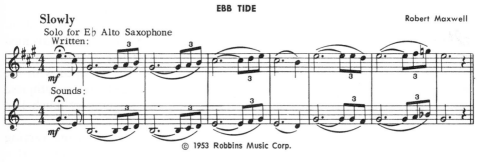

EBB TIDE

Robert Maxwell

© 1953 Robbins Music Corp.

b. To play sustained or moving harmony parts;

(1)

A MELODIC CARAVAN
(I'm In The Mood For Love)

Jimmy McHugh, Dorothy Fields

© 1935 (Renewal 1963) Robbins Music Corp.

(2)

SONG OF THE BAYOU

Rube Bloom

c. To play counter-melodies;

WHEN I GROW TOO OLD TO DREAM

Oscar Hammerstein II, Sigmund Romberg

CHAPTER THREE

THE BRASSES

In ancient times, people knew how to make horns that produced sounds when they blew them. The earliest were made from the horns of animals. Later, horns were made from straight metal tubes. Then, someone learned how to bend the long metal tube, and instruments similar to bugles were made.

The bugle, which has no keys or valves, plays only a few tones in the tonic chord. The bugle player is able to play these different tones by making his lips tighter for the high tones and looser for the low ones.

Ex. 51

THE BUGLE-TONES

do   so   do   mi   so

For many centuries, all of the brass instruments could play only those tones which could be made in this way. Then, extra pieces of tubing were fitted into the instruments in order to make them longer or shorter. The players could produce a different set of bugle-tones for each different length of tubing.

Still later, instead of adding extra pieces of tubing, someone found that two tubes could be made to slide over each other (something like a tele-scope). The player could then make the entire tube longer or shorter.

The modern trombone is made and played in this way. It has two U-shaped pieces, one of which fits over the other. The sliding piece is moved by the player, making the total length of the two tubes longer or shorter.

When a trombone player holds the slide in one of the positions, he is able to play any one of the bugle-tones that go with a tube of that length. The hand selects the position, and the lips select the tone.

Ex. 52

THE POSITIONS OF THE TROMBONE

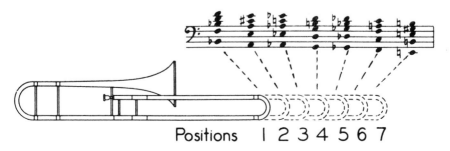

Positions   1 2 3 4 5 6 7

During the period 1800-1830, inventors in Europe learned how to put valves on brass instruments. When a valve is pressed down, it adds a specific length of tubing to the air-column within the instrument. Each valve or combination of valves provides the length of tubing with which a series of bugle-tones can be played.

By using his lips, a trumpet player can produce the following tones without using any of the valves:

Ex. 53

By pressing down the second (middle) valve, and using his lips, the player can produce the following tones:

Ex. 54

In a similar manner, the other valves may be used separately or in various combinations. The second valve lowers the pitch (of the series of bugle-tones) one half-step; the first valve, two half-steps; the third valve, three half-steps.

Ex. 55

FINGERING PLAN FOR TRUMPET

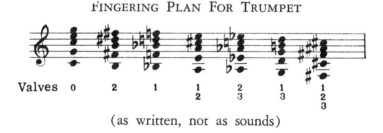

(as written, not as sounds)

The brass family includes the trumpet, French horn, trombone, and tuba. All of the brass instruments are very much like bugles, except that they have valves or slides so that they can make more tones of different pitch.

A characteristic of the brass instruments is that tone is produced on them by means of cup mouthpieces of various sizes and shapes. The player does not make a tone by blowing into the instrument. He places his lips against the mouthpiece, tightens the lips properly, and then blows gently, causing the lips to vibrate. The vibrating lips cause the air-column within the instrument to vibrate and make the tones that we hear.

MUTES AND MUTING

The tone color of the brass instruments may be altered, and their volume reduced, by means of mutes.

A straight mute for a trumpet is a cone-shaped device which fits into the bell of the instrument and changes the tone color so that it resembles that of the oboe. Other kinds of mutes, producing other tone colors, are available.

Several kinds of mutes are made for trombones. They are similar to those made for trumpets. Tuba mutes are not used as often as they could be.

Muting on the French horn has always meant that the player's right hand had to be placed in the bell of the horn much farther than in ordinary playing. This changed the tone color, reduced the volume, and required the player to use different fingerings. Horn mutes which change only the color and volume of the tone, but not the pitch, are now available. With these mutes, the player uses the regular fingerings.

When the composer wishes a brass player to use a mute, the part is marked "muted" or "con sordino". When the mute is to be removed, the indication is "open" or "senza sordino". Muted tones on the horn, also called stopped tones, are marked with a cross.

The composer or arranger must remember that it takes a little time for the player to insert or remove a mute. The player should be given some rests in his part so that he can make the change.

In the past, the use of mutes for trumpets and trombones was limited, to a large degree, to dance band playing. There is no reason, however, why these tone colors may not be used whenever suitable and appropriate.

THE TRUMPET AND THE CORNET

Trumpets and cornets are different in some ways, but for most purposes either one may be used. The statements which follow apply to both instruments in their modern forms.

The trumpet is made of a brass tube 4' 7½" long, coiled into an oblong shape. It has a small cup mouthpiece at one end and a cone-shaped bell at the other. It is fingered by means of three piston valves.

Music for the B♭ trumpet is usually written within the range shown below, but it sounds a whole-step lower. The closed notes indicate the practical school orchestra range.

Ex. 56

TRUMPET

WRITTEN   SOUNDS

The trumpet is the soprano of the brass family. It can play fairly rapid passages or slow, expressive melodies. Its tone is brilliant and penetrating, especially in the upper register. Trumpet players need to rest, now and then, during the music.

Music arranged for school orchestras usually has parts for first trumpet and for second trumpet. There is a trend, nowadays, toward having three trumpet parts. (Symphonic music may have three or four parts.)

When writing for any two like instruments, it is important that their parts be written in good duet style, using mainly thirds, sixths, augmented fourths, and diminished fifths. This is especially true when writing for two trumpets. These instruments are heard clearly in the orchestra, and their parts require careful attention.

The trumpet is very effective when playing figures, similar to bugle calls, based upon the intervals of a chord. It is also able to play effectively rather short scale passages, either diatonic or chromatic.

The trumpet is well adapted to playing rapidly repeated tones by means of double or triple tonguing. On the other hand, the trumpet is not very effective when playing trills.

Trumpets that are used in school orchestras are built in B♭. Some have an A slide. Most books on orchestration discuss the trumpet in A and advise its use when the orchestra is playing in certain keys: those having several sharps in the signature. This practice is not recommended, however, when writing for school orchestras.

When the trumpet is used with the A slide, it is less perfectly in tune. Since fingering is never a real problem on a brass instrument, trumpet players can learn their parts on a B♭ instrument, even though there are several sharps in the signature. The only problems are note reading and the use of less familiar fingerings.

Ex. 57

TRUMPET

(All of the following examples are shown as they sound.)
Trumpets may be used:
a. To play characteristic solos;

b. To play the principal melody with other instruments;

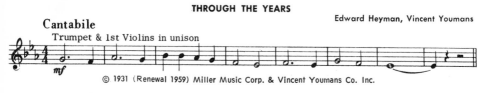

THROUGH THE YEARS

Edward Heyman, Vincent Youmans

Cantabile

Trumpet & 1st Violins in unison

© 1931 (Renewal 1959) Miller Music Corp. & Vincent Youmans Co. Inc.

c. To play rhythmic, staccato accompaniment figures;

TEMPTATION

Arthur Freed, Nacio Herb Brown

Beguine tempo

Violins

Trumpets

© 1933 (Renewal 1961) Metro-Goldwyn-Mayer Inc.   Copyright asgd. 1933 Robbins Music Corp. for U.S. & Canada

d. To play fanfare-like passages;

OUR DIRECTOR

F. E. Bigelow
Arr. Merle J. Isaac

(1) **Bright march tempo**

Violins

Trumpets

(2)

© 1953 Walter Jacobs Inc.

e. To play sustained harmony parts;

THE PRESIDENT'S LADY

Alfred Newman

Slowly

Violins

Trumpet (muted)

© 1953 Twentieth Century Music Corp.

f. To play passages with ornamental figuration;

A MELODIC CARAVAN
(Cuban Love Song)

Herbert Stothart, Jimmy McHugh, Dorothy Fields

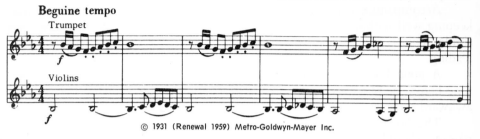

THE FRENCH HORN

The modern French horn in F consists of a brass tube, 12 feet long, coiled in a circular shape, with a small cup mouthpiece and a very large bell. Three rotary valves are operated by the player's left hand.

Music for the horn is usually written within the range shown below, but it sounds a perfect fifth lower. The closed notes indicate the practical range for school orchestras.

Ex. 58

HORN IN F

WRITTEN SOUNDS

The horn is the alto of the brass family. Its tone is generally smooth and mellow, and it blends well with all of the other instruments. Melodies, counter-melodies, and accompaniment parts are all effectively played by the horns.

In arranging music for school orchestras, it is customary to write for two or four horns. When writing for four horns, the parts usually dovetail or interlock. The first and third horns play the higher tones, and the second and fourth horns play the lower tones. The part for the third horn usually lies between the parts for the first and second horns.

Ex. 59

Horns in F

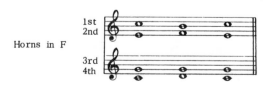

Many orchestras have only two horn players, so the first and second horn parts must contain the more important tones of the chords. The orchestration must sound complete with only two horn parts being played, though it will sound more full and rich with the four parts.

Accompaniment parts for the horns should not go too high nor too low, keeping well within the practical school range. Dominant seventh chords and similar chords should resolve according to the rules of harmony and voice leading.

A good horn part should be easy to sing. The player must think every tone before he plays it. Therefore, the part should be singable, and contain no awkward skips or unusual intervals.

The horn is a noble instrument, but not a particularly agile one. Fast passages should not be given to the horns.

At one time, horn parts were written without key signatures, and the necessary accidentals were placed as needed. There is no reason for following this custom. Horn parts, like those for all other instruments (except percussion instruments without definite pitch), should be written with key signatures.

Ex. 60

HORN

(All of the examples, except (a), are shown in actual pitch.)

Horns may be used:

a. To play characteristic solos;

OVER THE RAINBOW

E. Y. Harburg, Harold Arlen

© 1939 Leo Feist Inc.

b. To play the principal melody with other instruments;

BALLET PARISIEN

Jacques Offenbach
Arr. Merle J. Isaac

© 1955 Carl Fischer Inc.   Used by permission.

c. To play sustained harmony parts;

MEXICAN OVERTURE

Merle J. Isaac

© 1944 Carl Fischer Inc.   Used by permission.

d. To play counter-melodies;

RAMONA

L. Wolfe Gilbert, Mabel Wayne

Valse moderato

e. To play after-beat accompaniments;

(1)

VINCENT YOUMANS FANTASY
(Great Day)

Edward Eliscu, William Rose, Vincent Youmans

Brightly

(2)

NATIONAL EMBLEM

E. E. Bagley
Arr. Merle J. Isaac

March tempo

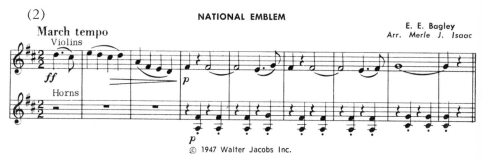

THE TROMBONE

The slide trombone differs from the other members of the brass family in one respect: it has no valves.

The trombone consists of 9 feet of brass tubing, bent to make a long, narrow instrument. Much of the tubing is made so that it slides back and forth upon itself, making a long tube or a short one. The player depends upon his ears to tell him where to stop the slide to get a tone of the correct pitch.

Music for the trombone is usually written within the range shown below, and it sounds as written. The closed notes indicate the practical range for school orchestras.

Ex. 61

TROMBONE

The trombone is the tenor of the brass family. Its tone has been described as noble and majestic. Generally, the instrument has much dignity. While the trombone is very effective as a solo instrument, it usually plays a harmony part in the orchestra. Three trombones played softly can provide a beautiful harmonic background.

Rapid scale passages are not suited to the instrument, but rapid repeated tones are effective.

Writing for the trombone's lower register requires care. The player should not be asked to shift to distant positions rapidly. With young players, it would be well to avoid the use of the sixth and seventh positions altogether. An example of awkward writing follows:

Ex. 62

Parts for three trombones may be written in close harmony in the middle and upper registers. Close harmony, however, should be avoided in the lower register.

Ex. 63

Ex. 64

TROMBONE

Trombones may be used:

a. To play characteristic solo passages;

VINCENT YOUMANS FANTASY
(Without A Song)

William Rose, Edward Eliscu, Vincent Youmans

Rather slowly, with expression

© 1929 (Renewal 1957) Miller Music Corp. & Vincent Youmans Co. Inc.

b. To play the principal melody with other instruments, in unison or in octaves;

THROUGH THE YEARS

Edward Heyman, Vincent Youmans

Cantabile
Trombone & Violins in octaves

© 1931 (Renewal 1959) Miller Music Corp. & Vincent Youmans Co. Inc.

50

c. To play sustained harmony parts;

MISSISSIPPI SUITE
(Father Of Waters)

Ferde Grofe

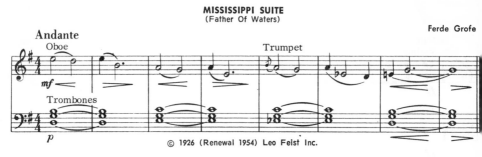

© 1926 (Renewal 1954) Leo Feist Inc.

d. To play counter-melodies;

MISSISSIPPI SUITE
(Mardi Gras)

Ferde Grofe

© 1926 (Renewal 1954) Leo Feist Inc.

e. To play rhythmic accompaniment parts;

TEMPTATION

Arthur Freed, Nacio Herb Brown

© 1933 (Renewal 1961) Metro-Goldwyn-Mayer Inc.   Copyright asgd. 1933 Robbins Music Corp. for U.S. & Canada

f. To play fanfare-like passages with trumpets or horns;

MISSISSIPPI SUITE
(Huckleberry Finn)

Ferde Grofe

© 1926 (Renewal 1954) Leo Feist Inc.

g. To play the bass part;

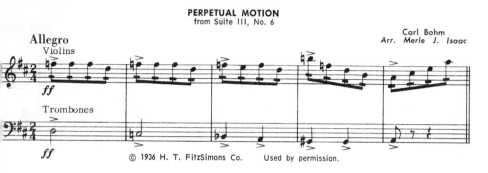

PERPETUAL MOTION
from Suite III, No. 6

Carl Bohm
Arr. Merle J. Isaac

© 1936 H. T. FitzSimons Co.   Used by permission.

THE TUBA

The tuba is the bass of the brass family. Over 18 feet of brass tubing, of large diameter, is used to make a BB♭ tuba.

The tuba that is used in the orchestra is usually coiled in much the same way as the trumpet, except that it is held with the bell pointing upward. It is called an upright tuba, and may be built in various keys. However, tubas are all non-transposing instruments and, in this respect, are no problem for the orchestrator.

Music for the tuba is usually written within the range given below. The closed notes indicate the practical school range. All tones sound as written.

Ex. 65

TUBA

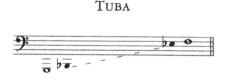

While the tuba can play a melody effectively, it is usually given a bass part. When played softly and sustained, the tuba has a beautiful organ-like quality of tone. When necessary, however, the tuba can match the brilliancy and force of the trumpets and trombones. A brass quartet of three trombones and a tuba playing loudly, in octaves, can be exciting and even frightening. Playing chorals softly, they are solemnly beautiful.

In some registers, the tuba is more agile than the trombone, since valves can be operated faster than slides. Large bass instruments, however, are not specially effective when they play rapid passages.

Tubas are most useful when they provide a bass for the brass section. In music arranged for school orchestras, the string bass notes are often cued in the tuba parts. Played softly, a tuba may help to fill out a small string bass section.

A school band has several tuba players, but a school orchestra, like a symphony orchestra, needs but one.

52

Ex. 66

TUBA

The Tuba may be used:

a. To play characteristic solo passages;

MUMMERS
Danse Grotesque

Moderato

John Merle

b. To play sustained bass parts;

THROUGH THE YEARS

Edward Heyman, Vincent Youmans

Cantabile
Trumpet

Tuba

rit. e dim.

c. To play rhythmic bass parts;

(1)

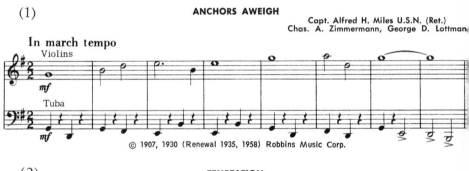

ANCHORS AWEIGH

Capt. Alfred H. Miles U.S.N. (Ret.)
Chas. A. Zimmermann, George D. Lottman

In march tempo
Violins

Tuba

(2)

TEMPTATION

Arthur Freed, Nacio Herb Brown

Moderate beguine tempo
Trumpet

Tuba

dim.

d. To play a melody with other instruments in unison or octaves;

LEGEND
(Tone Poem)

Merle J. Isaac

Allegro

CHAPTER FOUR

THE PERCUSSIONS

The percussion family of instruments includes the drums and all of the other instruments that are played by striking them with beaters or by striking them together.

Some of the percussion instruments have definite pitch and can play melodies or bass parts: xylophone, marimba, orchestra bells, and timpani.

Other percussion instruments have no definite pitch and play rhythm only: bass drum, snare drum, cymbals, castanets, tambourine, and triangle.

Almost every kind of percussion instrument has its own variety of beaters, made in different sizes and in different degrees of hardness. For example, there are heavy sticks and light sticks for the snare drum; hard sticks and soft sticks for the timpani. These different kinds of sticks help to make the music loud or soft, and change the color and quality of the tone being produced.

The timpani, xylophone, marimba, orchestra bells, and snare drum are played with two sticks or with two mallets. The player holds one stick in each hand, and uses first one and then the other.

On most percussion instruments, a single tap produces a tone of short duration. To play a long tone, it is necessary to play a roll. A roll is many short tones played close together so as to sound like one long tone.

On the timpani and xylophone, a roll is made by playing many rapid alternate taps: left, right, left, right (LRLR). This is a single-stroke roll.

On the snare drum, each hand plays two taps: LLRRLLRR. This is a double-stroke roll.

It is very important that the vibrating part of a percussion instrument is free to vibrate. If a triangle is hung loosely on a string and tapped with a beater (and the beater quickly taken away), it will vibrate freely and produce a clear, ringing tone. If the triangle is touched by the hand or by some other object, or if the beater is not quickly withdrawn, the tone will be a dull thud.

School orchestras usually have two or more players in their percussion sections. Each player may be called upon to play several different percussion instruments at different times during the playing of a composition. Usually there are two printed parts, marked "Timpani" and "Drums". The timpani part may include passages for the xylophone or orchestra bells if there are no notes for the timpani to be played at the same time. The drum part contains the notes for all of the various percussion instruments having indefinite pitch and may also include passages for the xylophone and bells.

Music for the percussion instruments having definite pitch is written much as music is written for the other orchestral instruments. Either a G clef or an F clef is used, with key and time signatures. The music sounds as written for the timpani, an octave higher for the xylophone, and two octaves higher for the bells.

Ex. 67

TIMPANI

Ex. 68

XYLOPHONE

ROMANY LIFE
from "The Fortune Teller"

Victor Herbert
Arr. Merle J. Isaac

© 1955 Belwin Inc.   Used by permission.

Rolls are written in two ways, as shown in Ex. 69, but the first way is preferred. A roll consists of the rapid reiteration of tones having the same pitch. A trill consists of the rapid alternation of two tones having different pitch, either a step or a half-step apart.

Ex. 69

THE ROLL

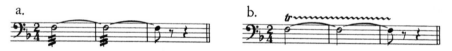

If a roll is to be a continuous one, the notes should be tied, as shown at (a) in Ex. 70. The notation at (b) indicates a new attack in each measure, with a slight separation between the tones.

Ex. 70

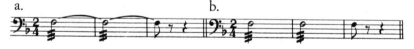

Music for the percussion instruments having indefinite pitch is sometimes written in conductor's scores with a single line for each instrument, as in Ex. 71.

Ex. 71

A PERCUSSION PASSAGE
as it might be written in the full score

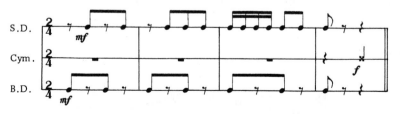

The drum parts given to the players, however, are written on a regular five line staff, with an F clef and a time-signature (but no key signature), as in Ex. 72.

Ex. 72

A PERCUSSION PASSAGE
as it would be written in the player's part

The composer or arranger who writes for school orchestras should keep in mind the fact that there are usually several drummers in an orchestra, and that they want to play. Drummers do not enjoy sitting and counting rests for long periods.

This does not mean that the composer should write an unmusical score with loud drum parts where they are uncalled for. It does mean, however, that the writer must use his musical ingenuity, and put a few triangle notes or a soft cymbal roll here and there, where suitable, so as to keep the drummers interested in the music.

Furthermore, soft, colorful, rhythmic percussion tones, now and then, can heighten the listener's interest and enjoyment. Quite often, the percussion part should be felt, rather than heard. It should never be obtrusive or noisy.

THE TIMPANI
(Kettledrums)

A kettledrum consists of a large copper kettle, a tightly stretched calfskin head, tension rods for tuning, and a pair of sticks. Musicians usually call the kettledrums "timpani".

Timpani have definite pitch. They are tuned to certain notes in the music, usually a bass part, such as the tonic and dominant tones (the first and fifth tones in the scale). Formerly, the players had to turn six hand screws when they changed the pitch of a drum. Today, many players have pedal timpani, and the pitch is raised or lowered by means of pedals. Making the head tighter raises the pitch. Making the head looser lowers the pitch.

Symphony orchestras may have three or more timpani, though always one player. School orchestras usually have a pair of timpani which can produce the tones indicated below.

Ex. 73

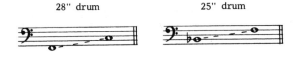

28" drum   25" drum

A timpani player needs a little time to tune his drums at the beginning of a piece of music and, if there are pitch changes during the composition, he needs time to change and check. Too many changes are difficult. The player must tune his drums while the rest of the orchestra is playing, possibly in quite another key. He must have a good ear.

Since the timpani player can read music and has a good ear for pitch relationships, his music should be written with a key signature, the same as all other parts, except those for the percussion instruments without definite pitch.

Ex. 74

TIMPANI

Characteristic Passages for the Timpani:

LEGEND
(Tone Poem)

Merle J. Isaac

LEGEND
(Tone Poem)

Merle J. Isaac

JEANNINE
(I Dream of Lilac Time)

L. Wolfe Gilbert, Nathaniel Shilkret

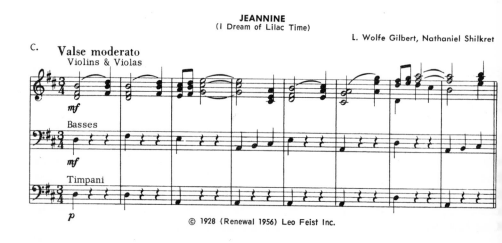

d.

THROUGH THE YEARS

Edward Heyman, Vincent Youmans

THE BASS DRUM

A bass drum consists of a wooden shell, two calfskin heads, tension rods, and a beater.

The shell is a hollow cylinder from 14 to 18 inches in depth.

The heads are from 20 to 40 inches in diameter.

A bass drum beater has a ball at one end made either of lamb's wool (for the softer tones) or of felt (for the louder tones). Occasionally, a beater has a head at each end of the stick. This type may be used to play a roll on the bass drum.

The pitch of the bass drum is indefinite. The larger drums give louder tones.

Ordinarily, music for the bass drum is written in the first space of the staff, using the F clef, with stems down. Unless the music indicates otherwise, a half-note is played louder than a quarter-note.

Ex. 75

A BASS DRUM PASSAGE

The bass drum is used to accent the rhythm (as in a march) or to produce special effects (such as cannon shots or thunder rolls). The bass drum has a wide dynamic range from *ppp* to *fff*. Everyone is familiar with the loud tones of the bass drum. However, the soft tones deserve greater use. They can be mysterious, ominous, or merely provide a slight emphasis to the rhythm. One bass drum is adequate for even the largest orchestra.

THE SNARE DRUM

A snare drum consists of a wooden or metal shell, two tightly stretched calfskin heads, tension rods, snares, and a pair of sticks.

The shell is a short, hollow cylinder from 6½ to 8 inches deep. (There are also parade drums which are from 10 to 12 inches deep.)

The drum heads are from 14 to 15 inches in diameter. The head on the upper end of the drum is the batter head. The head on the lower end is the snare head. Stretched across the snare head are the snares, made of gut or wire.

When the player strikes the batter head, the snares rattle against the snare head. This gives the snare drum its crisp, brittle tone. For special effects, the snares may be loosened. The drum then sounds dull and hollow, something like an Indian tom-tom.

Two hardwood sticks about 16 inches long, with small oval heads, are used to play single strokes, double-stroke rolls, and a great variety of rhythmic figures.

Music for the snare drum is usually written in the third space of the staff, using the F clef, with stems up.

Ex. 76

SNARE DRUM PASSAGES

In the above example, (a) illustrates a characteristic snare drum passage without rolls; (b) is another passage from a march making use of short rolls; (c) illustrates the continuous roll, while (d) indicates a series of accented, separated rolls.

The snare drum should not be used too much, except in a march, or it will become tiresome to the listener. Used sparingly and judiciously, it can intensify the rhythmic quality of the music. Or, with a long roll, it can heighten the excitement of an approaching climax.

Dance drummers make considerable use of the wire brushes on the snare drum. These add quiet rhythm, and can be used freely with music in the popular style.

CYMBALS

Cymbals are round saucer-like disks made of brass or bronze. They are from 12 to 20 inches in diameter. The leather strap handles are loose enough to let the cymbals vibrate freely.

Cymbals are often used in pairs, the player holding one in each hand. The cymbals are struck together, with a glancing blow, as they slide past each other. This can produce a loud crash or a soft swish. The tone may be permitted to ring indefinitely or it may be choked (stopped) by touching the vibrating cymbals to the clothing of the player.

Sometimes only one cymbal is used. It may be suspended and struck with a soft timpani stick (sounding like a gong). A roll may be played upon it with a pair of snare drum sticks (sounding something like a roll on a triangle), or a pair of timpani sticks (sounding mysterious when *pp*, exciting when *ff*). Wire brushes, too, may be used to strike the cymbal to produce a soft novel effect.

Music for the cymbals is usually written in the second space of the staff, using the F clef. Ordinary noteheads may be used, or special noteheads that are either diamond shaped or like x's, as shown in Ex. 77.

Ex. 77

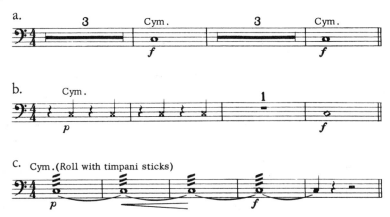

Cymbals, used sparingly, add much to music. Played softly, they add color and brilliance. Played loudly, they add volume and excitement.

THE CASTANETS

Castanets are made of two small pieces of hard wood, shaped something like oyster shells. They are held in the palm of the hand, and clicked together by the fingers.

For orchestral use, one or two pairs of castanets are fastened to a handle. When the handle is shaken, the castanets make a dry, clicking sound that suggests Spanish music.

Music for the castanets is usually written in the top space of the staff, using the F clef.

Ex. 78

CASTANET RHYTHMS

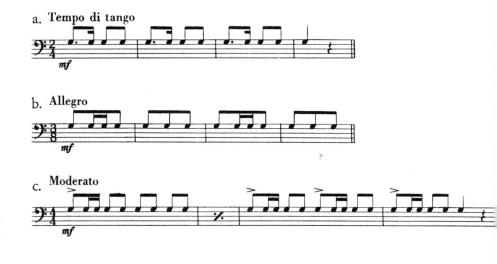

a. Tempo di tango

b. Allegro

c. Moderato

THE TAMBOURINE

The tambourine is a small drum, 8 or 10 inches in diameter, with a narrow wooden shell, and only one calfskin head. Many small metal disks called jingles, are placed in slots all around the shell.

When the tambourine is struck, the head makes a short percussive sound, and the jingles clash like tiny cymbals. When the tambourine is shaken, the jingles make a continuous rattling sound that is pleasant and musical. Sometimes the player rubs the head with his thumb and makes a sound something like a drum roll with jingles.

We think of Spanish, Italian, or Gipsy music when we hear a tambourine, though it has other uses.

Music for the tambourine is usually written in the top space of the staff, using the F clef.

Ex. 79

TAMBOURINE RHYTHMS

a. Allegro

b. Andante

THE TRIANGLE

The triangle is a steel rod that has been bent into the shape of a triangle, but open in one corner. The 6, 8, and 10 inch sizes are most commonly used.

The triangle beater is a small steel rod.

The triangle is held loosely with a string, and struck lightly with a beater. It makes a bright, bell-like tone, without definite pitch.

A roll may be played on the triangle by shaking the beater back and forth in one corner, striking two sides alternately.

An occasional triangle tone, played softly, adds brightness to the music. A triangle roll, in a loud passage, adds excitement. To be used effectively, the triangle must be used sparingly.

Music for the triangle is usually written in the top space of the staff, using the F clef, with stems up.

Ex. 80

THE GONG

The gong, or tam-tam, is made from hammered brass or bronze. It is circular, from 20 to 30 inches in diameter. It has a narrow edge turned at right angles to the gong itself, giving it somewhat the shape of a top for a very large jar.

The gong is hung in a special frame so that it may vibrate freely. It may be struck with a bass drum beater. It has no definite pitch.

When played softly, the tone is very solemn and mysterious. When played loudly, the gong creates a feeling of horror or great excitement. We often associate the instrument with China or other countries in the Far East.

Music for the gong is usually written in the second space of the staff, using the F clef. To be effective, the part should consist of few notes, and they should be of rather long duration.

Ex. 81

PERCUSSION

Some of the ways in which percussion instruments may be used are shown in the following illustrations:

ANCHORS AWEIGH

Capt. Alfred H. Miles U.S.N. (Ret.)
Chas. A. Zimmermann, George D. Lottman

OUR DIRECTOR

F. E. Bigelow
Arr. Merle J. Isaac

TEMPTATION

Arthur Freed, Nacio Herb Brown

c. **Moderate beguine tempo**

VINCENT YOUMANS FANTASY
(Drums In My Heart)

Edward Heyman, Vincent Youmans

d. **Brightly**

Solo for the percussion section — All other instruments tacet.

BALLET PARISIEN

Jacques Offenbach
Arr. Merle J. Isaac

e. **Allegro**

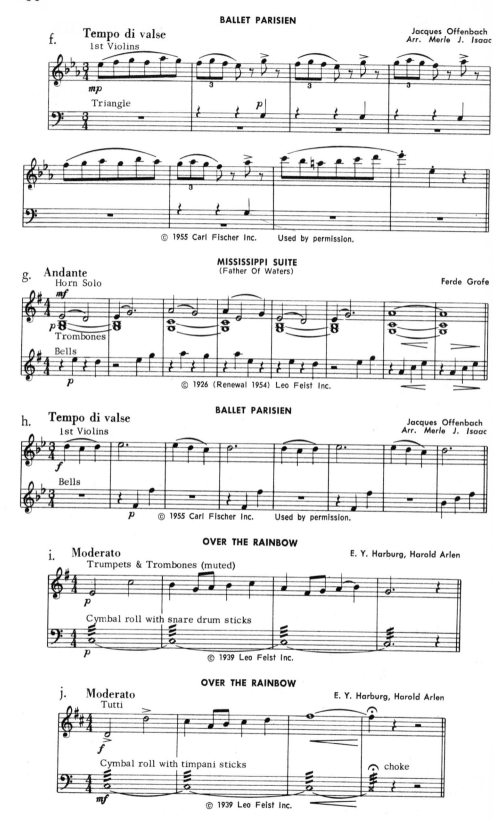

BALLET PARISIEN

f. Tempo di valse
1st Violins

Jacques Offenbach
Arr. Merle J. Isaac

© 1955 Carl Fischer Inc. Used by permission.

MISSISSIPPI SUITE
(Father Of Waters)

g. Andante
Horn Solo

Ferde Grofe

Trombones

Bells

© 1926 (Renewal 1954) Leo Feist Inc.

BALLET PARISIEN

h. Tempo di valse
1st Violins

Jacques Offenbach
Arr. Merle J. Isaac

Bells

© 1955 Carl Fischer Inc. Used by permission.

OVER THE RAINBOW

i. Moderato
Trumpets & Trombones (muted)

E. Y. Harburg, Harold Arlen

Cymbal roll with snare drum sticks

© 1939 Leo Feist Inc.

OVER THE RAINBOW

j. Moderato
Tutti

E. Y. Harburg, Harold Arlen

Cymbal roll with timpani sticks

choke

© 1939 Leo Feist Inc.

THE XYLOPHONE, MARIMBA, AND ORCHESTRA BELLS

These instruments are somewhat similar in appearance. All consist of bars of graduated sizes and of definite pitch, arranged like the black and white keys of the piano. However, there is one big difference: the bars of the xylophone and marimba are made of wood; the bars of the orchestra bells are made of steel.

The mallets used in playing these instruments are similar. The handles are rather flexible, and the heads may be made of plastic, rubber, or yarn. On all three instruments, the manner of holding the mallets and of striking the bars is quite similar.

The tone of the xylophone is dry and brittle. Each tone is very short. To give the effect of a long tone, the player must play a roll. Music for the xylophone is usually written within the range given below, but it sounds an octave higher.

Ex. 83

A xylophone passage usually consists of many short notes, and it is likely to be fast.

Ex. 84

RUSSIAN SAILORS' DANCE
from "The Red Poppy"

Reinhold Glière
Arr. Merle J. Isaac

Più mosso

f

© 1940 Carl Fischer Inc.   Used by permission.

The tone of the marimba is smooth and mellow. Beautiful effects are obtained by playing three or four different tones at one time, using three or four mallets.

When the marimba is used as part of the orchestra, not as a solo instrument, its part is usually fairly slow. Music for the marimba is written in the G clef.

Ex. 85

LATIN-AMERICAN FANTASY

Clifford P. Lillya, Merle J. Isaac

Tempo di valse lento

mf

© 1943 Carl Fischer Inc.   Used by permission.

The tone of the orchestra bells, also called glockenspiel, is like that of other bells: clear and ringing. Each tone sounds for a little while, after being struck, and rapid playing on bells becomes blurred. Rolls are playable on the bells, but they are not always effective.

Music for the orchestra bells is usually written within the range given below, and it sounds two octaves higher.

Ex. 86

Passages written for the orchestra bells are likely to be fairly slow, as in the following example.

Ex. 87

CSARDAS

V. Monti
Arr. Merle J. Isaac

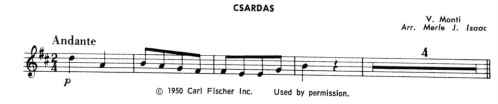

© 1950 Carl Fischer Inc.   Used by permission.

CHAPTER FIVE

NOTATION

Every student of orchestration has read music extensively. He has seen and understood the many symbols and characters used in the notation of music. He has written many of them in his study of harmony and counterpoint.

But reading music and writing music are two different skills, and the writing of musical notation, as it is used in orchestration, requires special study. A composer or an arranger who wishes to have his music played, and played well, must be certain that his manuscript is clearly and correctly written.

School musicians find it difficult to read music in manuscript form. If the manuscript resembles engraved music, they will read it more easily and play it much better.

Professional musicians are annoyed with inaccurate and illegible manuscript. It wastes precious rehearsal time and requires the players to give more attention to note reading (or note guessing) than to musical performance.

GUIDING PRINCIPLES

1. Manuscript should never be crowded.
2. Manuscript should resemble printed music as much as possible.
3. When a sign or symbol has two or more forms, use the familiar form found in engraved music, unless it is too difficult for manuscript use.

MANUSCRIPT PAPER

Manuscript paper, used for writing music, is a fairly heavy paper that takes ink or pencil and withstands erasures. It is usually ruled with music staves on both sides.

A page may have from 8 to 29 staves (called lines). Sometimes clefs and braces are printed on the paper, making it especially suitable for piano, voice and piano, orchestra score, or band score.

Several sizes are available, the following being the most commonly used:

Concert — Large	$10\frac{1}{2}$ x $13\frac{1}{2}$
Concert	$9\frac{1}{2}$ x $12\frac{1}{2}$
Octavo	$6\frac{3}{4}$ x $10\frac{1}{2}$
Quickstep — Band	$6\frac{3}{4}$ x $5\frac{1}{2}$

For orchestra scores, the large size with many lines should be used. For orchestra parts, piano music, and almost everything except scores, the concert size with 12 lines is generally satisfactory.

Each sheet of manuscript paper is folded and includes four pages. One may purchase six sheets (24 pages), a quire (24 sheets, 96 pages), or larger quantities.

PEN OR PENCIL?

When writing early drafts of a score, use a soft pencil, and have a good pencil eraser handy. When writing a score for a conductor and the separate parts for the players, write in ink. Writers use different kinds of ink, but all of them are *black!* Some writers use a three-point music pen; others use a stub pen. A little experimenting with pens will be helpful.

ERASURES AND CORRECTIONS

A single-edge razor blade is a good ink eraser. When a wrong note has been written, write in the correct note and let the ink dry. Then, using the razor blade, carefully scrape away the ink of the wrong note.

When an extensive error has been made, it is easier and neater to cover the mistake with music paper pasted in place. (Rubber cement makes an excellent adhesive.) There is a convenient gummed music tape which may also be used for making corrections. The tape is pasted in place and, after the paper has dried, the correct notes or other symbols may be written on it.

NOTES

Ex. 88

A whole-note in engraved music usually resembles (a) in the example above. It is *not* the same as the head of the half-note.

In manuscript, however, the whole-note shown at (b) is quite satisfactory. It is easier to write, and its meaning is clear.

The size of notes (both the note-heads and the stems) is determined by the size of the spaces of the staff. Note-heads should be just large enough to fill a space of the staff. When too small, they are difficult to read. When too large, they cover both a line and a space, and cannot be read at all. Note-heads should be uniform in size.

Both the white notes and the black notes have oval heads of the same size, inclined at the same angle. There is a tendency, when writing music manuscript, to make the black note-heads slightly smaller. This is not objectionable if the manuscript is clear and legible. However, note-heads must never become dots!

STEMS

Ex. 89

(The following statements, and many others in this chapter, apply mainly when one part only is written on a staff.)

Some stems go up, and some go down. This is done to keep the note-head and its stem on the staff as much as possible, making the notation better looking and easier to read.

When a single note-head is below the middle line of the staff (a), the stem goes up from the right side of the note-head.

When a single note-head is above the middle line of the staff (c), the stem goes down from the left side of the note-head.

There is a difference of opinion concerning the direction of the stem on a single note-head placed on the middle line (b). In engraved music, the stem usually goes down.

Stems are always vertical.

Stems vary in length, depending on conditions. Ordinarily, a stem equals three spaces and is an octave in length. Sixteenth-notes and thirty-second-notes, having two or three flags (d), require longer stems.

Notes written with leger lines (e) usually have longer stems. These stems extend to the middle line of the staff.

NOTES ON ADJACENT DEGREES

Ex. 90

Notes written on adjacent degrees of the staff are illustrated above.

When adjacent notes are on the same stem (a), the upper note is placed at the right.

When adjacent notes have separate stems (b), the upper note is placed at the left.

STEMS ON CHORDS

Ex. 91

When two or more notes are written as a chord, the stem is written up or down according to the requirement of the majority of the notes in the chord.

If most of the notes are below the middle line of the staff (a), the stem goes up.

If most of the notes are above the middle line (b), the stem goes down.

Notice the placement of notes on adjacent degrees of the staff (a) and (b).

FLAGS

Ex. 92

Flags (hooks), used with single notes shorter than quarter-notes, are always placed on the right side of the stem.

If the arranger finds it difficult to draw the wavy flags found in printed music, a straight flag at 45° (d) may be used.

BEAMS

Ex. 93

In vocal music (a), notes shorter than quarter-notes are usually written with flags.

In instrumental music (b), such notes are written with beams whenever possible.

Ex. 94

The grouping of notes with beams is based upon rhythmic units: the beats of the measure.

When most of the note-heads in a group are on the middle line or above (a), the stems go down.

When most of the note-heads are below the middle line (b), the stems go up. An exception to this rule is made if one of the note-heads (c) is at a great distance from the middle line.

Beams are also used with notes of mixed values (e). The short stroke for a single sixteenth-note is placed on the side of the stem near the longer note (f).

RESTS

Ex. 95

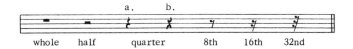

The whole-rest is placed *below* the fourth line. It is used to fill an entire measure no matter what the time-signature may be.

The half-rest is placed *above* the third line.

The whole-rest and the half-rest look very much alike. Remember that the whole-rest is *under* the line, while the half-rest is *over* the line.

The quarter-rest has two forms. Form (a) is used in engraved music. Form (b) is often used in manuscript. It is like the letter Z, but backwards!

The hooks on the shorter rests correspond in number to the flags on the shorter notes. Hooks on rests are placed to the left of the stem.

Unlike the stems of notes which are vertical, stems on the shorter rests slant. And they always go down.

Ex. 96

Orchestra players often have rests of one measure or of two, three, or more consecutive measures. Such long rests are written as shown above.

TIES

Ex. 97

A tie is a curved line, somewhat heavy in the middle and light at the ends, as an archer's bow.

The tie is ordinarily placed on the side of the note-heads opposite the stems, though (d) shows a necessary exception.

DOTTED NOTES

Ex. 98

Ex. 98 shows how a note may be made longer by using a dot or a tie or both.

A dotted half-note, shown at (a), may be thought of as a short method of writing a half-note tied to a quarter-note (b).

Similarly, measures (c) and (d) show how an eighth-note may be lengthened with a dot or with a tie.

A double dotted note (e) represents three tied notes (f). The notation at (g) is the easiest to read.

Ex. 99

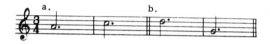

When the note-head is in a space (a), the dot is placed in the same space. When the note-head is on a line (b), the dot is placed in the space above.

Ex. 100

Dotted notes should not be used if there is another way of writing the rhythm that is easier to read, one that gives the eye a better picture of the rhythm.

The time figure shown at (e) is satisfactory in dance music if it occurs many times and the players become familiar with it. However, the notation shown at (f) is easier to read and play.

DOTTED RESTS

Ex. 101

While it is correct to write dotted rests (the dot makes the rest half again as long), they make note reading more difficult, and are seldom used. Their use should be avoided, and rests should be lengthened as shown in (b) and (d).

CLEFS

Ex. 102

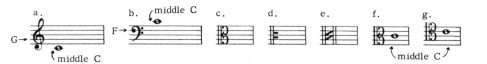

Three kinds of clefs are in common use. Each clef must have the right shape and be placed on the right line of the staff.

The treble or G clef (a) designates the second line as G above middle C. The bass or F clef (b) designates the fourth line as F below middle C. There is little variation, if any, in the form and use of these two clefs.

The C clef, however, presents difficulties. It is less familiar, is harder to draw, and is movable. Engravers use the form of the C clef shown at (c). Examples (d) and (e) show forms of the C clef which are acceptable in manuscript music. These forms are easier to draw, and their meaning is clear.

The C clef shown at (f) is an alto clef, designating the middle line as middle C. This clef is used by the viola.

The C clef shown at (g) is a tenor clef, designating the fourth line as middle C. This clef is used occasionally in music written for the cello, bassoon, and trombone.

CHROMATIC SIGNS

Ex. 103

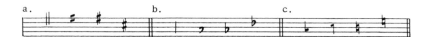

A sharp (a) consists of two light vertical lines, two heavy slanting lines, and the center area which designates the line or space being affected. The vertical lines are a little more than two spaces long. The heavier slanting lines are much shorter.

A flat (b) resembles a small letter "b". Here, too, the open space within the flat corresponds to a note-head in designating the line or space affected. The vertical line is about two spaces long. The curved portion is much like the right half of a heart (as found on a valentine).

The natural sign or cancel (c) is written with two strokes: a sort of "L" and an inverted "L". The center area must be correctly placed on the staff. The light vertical lines are a little over two spaces long. The heavy slanting lines are about one space long. It is interesting to notice the similarities between the sharp and the natural.

KEY-SIGNATURES

Ex. 104

The group of sharps or flats placed after the clef at the beginning of each staff is called the key-signature.

The sharps or flats must be placed in the right octave (as shown above).

They must follow in the right order.

They are never placed over or under one another. Each is well to the right of the one before it.

A sharp or a flat in a key-signature affects all of the notes on its line or in its space, and all of the octaves of that line or space, throughout an entire composition, or section of a composition, until the key is changed.

Memorize the key-signatures of seven sharps and seven flats and you will know *all* the key-signatures. Notice that the seven letter-names of the sharps and the flats follow in the same sequence, but in reverse order.

KEY-SIGNATURE CANCELLATIONS

Ex. 105

Key changes occur within most compositions. If the new key-signature contains *more* sharps or *more* flats than the previous key-signature (a) and (b), it is quite satisfactory to draw a light double-bar and write the new signature.

But sometimes the new key-signature contains *fewer* sharps or flats than the previous one, or the key changes from sharps to flats or vice versa. In any of these cases, it is customary to emphasize the key change by cancelling sharps or flats in the old signature before writing the new signature.

In the example above, (c) (d) and (e) are all correct, but (e) is the preferred form.

Engravers plan their layout so that a key-signature change usually occurs at the end of a line. The beginning of the next line, then, shows the new key-signature without the cancellation.

ACCIDENTALS

Chromatic signs which occur in music (exclusive of those actually in the key-signature) are called accidentals. A sharp or a flat in a key-signature has a wide influence, but an accidental's influence is quite limited. An accidental affects only those notes within its measure which follow on the same line or space. An accidental does not affect the notes in other octaves.

Bar-lines cancel accidentals. (An exception will be discussed later.) However, to remind the player that the accidentals have been cancelled, or to remove any doubts in his mind, courtesy accidentals are often used if the same note reappears in the next measure or two.

Ex. 106

A player sight-reading Ex. 106 could not be sure whether the F in the third measure is F sharp or F natural. True, as it is written, the bar-line cancels the previous F sharp and therefore the note should be read as F natural. But the player would be justified, from the context, in thinking that the copyist had omitted the sharp by mistake. Whenever the notation leaves doubt and uncertainty in a player's mind, the notation should be clarified.

The second notation (b) shows the use of a courtesy accidental. The natural sign in the third measure clarifies the notation and gives the player confidence.

Ex. 107

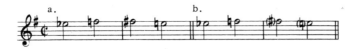

Courtesy (cautionary) accidentals are sometimes placed in parentheses, which make their function clear. The accidentals are not needed, but serve as reminders.

The parentheses, being additional signs, may confuse the eye. For this reason, parentheses should *not* be used unless they are needed to clarify the notation.

In the above example, (a) is easier to read than (b).

Ex. 108

The example above illustrates an exception to the rule that "bar-lines cancel accidentals". The modified rule may be stated, "A bar-line cancels an accidental unless the note affected is tied over the bar-line into the following measure".

Ex. 109

The above example illustrates the difference between a chromatic sign in a key-signature and one that is an accidental. In the second measure, for instance, the C♯ in the key-signature affects both the high C and the low C.

In the third measure, the C♮ affects only the C in the third space, and has no effect on the low C♯.

Since this is unusual and confusing, the third measure of (a) should be written as shown at (b) with a courtesy accidental.

Ex. 110

When accidentals are used with chords, there is likely to be a problem of vertical alignment. Unless the notes of the chord are well separated (a fifth or more), it may be impossible to place the accidentals in perfect vertical alignment. Instead, as shown in the example above, they must be placed alternately in two vertical columns.

When two accidentals are used with notes fairly close together, the lower accidental is usually placed to the left (1, 2, 8).

When there are three accidentals, two are usually placed near the notes, with the third one to the left (4, 6, 7).

Four accidentals can usually be placed in two columns (10).

Accidentals take up as much space on the staff, horizontally, as notes. This must be considered when planning layouts.

BARS AND DOUBLE-BARS

Ex. 111

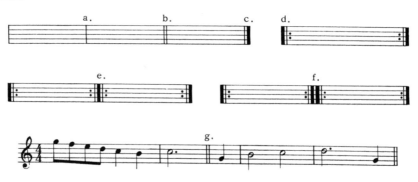

A bar is a light vertical line (a) drawn across a staff to divide it into measures.

A double-bar consisting of two light lines (b) is used to indicate the end of a section of music within a composition.

A double-bar consisting of one light bar and one heavy bar (c) is used to indicate the end of a composition.

This form of the double-bar with two dots (d) is used at the beginning and end of a strain to indicate that the strain is to be repeated. Notice that there are left and right forms.

When each of two successive strains is to be repeated, the double-bar between them may take either of the forms shown at (e) and (f).

It is correct, but somewhat confusing, to have a double-bar placed within a measure (g) where one section ends and another begins. Unless one of the sections is repeated, this use of the double-bar can be avoided merely by omitting it.

Ex. 112

A strain that is repeated except for the cadence may be written as shown in Ex. 112 with a first ending and a second ending. This notation indicates that the measures are to be played in the following order: 1-2-3-4-1-2-3-5. The first ending may be one or two measures long.

This notation saves both time for the writer and space on the printed page. However, it adds to the difficulty of reading, especially sight-reading.

Except in simple music, such as marches, it is best to avoid the use of repeat signs.

TIME-SIGNATURES

Ex. 113

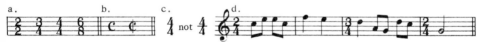

The time-signature (also called measure-sign, measure-signature, and meter-signature) is written after the key-signature only once: at the beginning of a composition. Later, if the meter changes, another time-signature is written (again, only once).

The two numbers in a time-signature (a) are not a fraction. They refer to two quite different things.

The upper number indicates the number of beats in each measure.

The lower number indicates the kind of a note that gets one beat.

While the signs for "common time" and "cut time" (alla breve), as shown at (b), are widely used and generally understood, they merely duplicate the time-signatures $\frac{4}{4}$ and $\frac{2}{2}$. These signs can be replaced by the more uniform and specific numerals.

When a time-signature is placed on a staff, the middle line of the staff happens to separate the numbers. When a time-signature is written without a staff (c), there should be no line between the numbers.

Ordinarily, a light double-bar precedes a time-signature which occurs at the beginning of a section within a composition. However, no double-bar is needed when the time changes frequently during a passage, as shown at (d).

THE NOTATION OF RHYTHM

Music should be written so that it may be read easily, quickly, and correctly.

The notation of rhythm in its simpler forms is not difficult. It is concerned largely with the selection and spacing of the symbols of duration: notes and rests.

1. Those symbols must be selected which will most clearly picture the rhythm.

2. The symbols must be correctly spaced, within the measure, so as to help the eye interpret the relative time values indicated.

Ex. 114

THE NOTATION OF RHYTHM IS BASED UPON RHYTHMIC UNITS: THE BEATS OF THE MEASURE.

In the above example, the small quarter-notes represent the beats of the measure.

In measures (a) (b) and (c), the large quarter-notes and eighth-notes follow very closely the rhythm of the small quarter-notes, the beats of the measure.

In measure (d), the third beat is not clearly visible. Measure (e) shows the same rhythm, using a tie instead of a dot, and the rhythmic picture is much clearer.

Measure (f) violates the same principle as (d), but it is acceptable because it is simple and common. Rhythmically, measure (g) is better.

Measure (h) illustrates a very poor notation. It is difficult to read. It fails to picture the rhythm. Measures (i) (j) and (k) indicate the same rhythm, more clearly expressed, using dots, ties, and a combination of both. The last measure gives the best notation for the rhythm.

Ex. 115

The examples in $\frac{6}{8}$ time illustrate even more vividly the principle that the notation of rhythm must be based upon rhythmic units: the beats of the measure. In $\frac{6}{8}$ time, at moderate or fast tempos, there are two beats in each measure. In the example above, these two beats are indicated by the small, dotted quarter-notes.

Measures (a) and (b) follow the rhythm of the beats very closely.

Measures (c) through (h) show wrong and right notations.

Measures (c), (e) and (g) are correct for $\frac{3}{4}$ time, but not for $\frac{6}{8}$ time.

Ex. 116

When the notation of rhythm requires rests as well as notes, they must conform to the same principles of rhythmic grouping.

In examples (a) (c) (e) and (g), all of the measures are mathematically correct: the values of the notes and rests add up to the correct number of beats in each measure. But not all of the measures make the rhythm clear to the eye.

The best notation makes the music look like it sounds, and helps the eye to read the rhythm at sight, quickly and correctly.

Correct notation promotes correct performance.

SPACING

Having selected the symbols that most clearly picture the rhythm of the music, placing them on paper becomes the next problem. If the player is to read the notes quickly and correctly, the notes and rests must be correctly placed and spaced within the measures.

Ex. 117

In Ex. 117, (a) is written on the basis of equal space for every beat. (The dots represent the beats of the measure.) If a quarter-note is given horizontal space on the staff equal to a quarter of an inch, a half-note gets half an inch, and a whole-note gets an inch. This method of spacing is quite logical. The rhythm is easy to read. In a simple score, this spacing is practical and desirable, and should be used.

The main objection to its use in the orchestra parts is that it wastes paper: a whole-note does not really need so much space.

Ex. 117 (b) is written on the basis of equal space for every *note*. Here, a whole-note or a sixteenth-note receives the same amount of horizontal space on the staff. (The bar-lines, of course, enter into the problem of spacing.) This method of spacing is difficult to read. The eye does not get a true picture of the rhythm of the music. In a score, with different parts having at the same time notes of different value, this method would be not at all suitable.

Ex. 117 (c) illustrates the kind of spacing used by engravers and writers of good manuscript. This method of spacing lies between the one which gives equal space for every *beat* (a) and the one which gives equal space for every *note* (b). The spacing is relatively proportionate, but not mathematically exact.

All notes of equal value receive equal space on the staff (other things being equal). Longer notes get more space than shorter notes. However, a whole-note does not get four times as much space as a quarter-note. It gets enough more space to enable the eye to recognize the relationship.

The amount of space given to the notes is determined, in part, by the kind of notes in the measure. If one passage consists largely of quarter-notes and eighth-notes, and another passage is largely quarter-notes and half-notes, the actual space given to the quarter-notes in the two cases will not be the same.

VERTICAL ALIGNMENT

When notes and rests are written on a staff, they must be properly spaced. When notes and rests are written in a score, there is another problem: vertical alignment. This problem must also be considered whenever two or more parts are written on one staff. Spacing and vertical alignment are two aspects of the same problem, that of helping the eye to interpret the written symbols.

Ex. 118

A note or a rest is placed at the left end of its allotted space, not in the center. Exceptions:

1. a whole-note in a single note part, but not in the score, may be placed midway between the left end and the center;

2. a whole-rest, in score or part, is usually placed in the center of the measure.

When two parts are written on one staff, notes that are sounded together must be placed exactly above and below each other. Examples (c) and (d) show the right and wrong placing of the whole-note.

Ex. 119

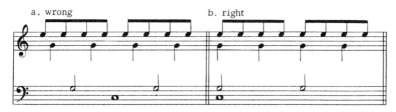

In score writing, it is very important that each note be placed at the left end of its allotted space. Notes that begin sounding together must be written in vertical alignment.

Ex. 119 (a) shows how a four-part score looks when each of the notes is placed in the middle of its allotted space. The illustration at (b) places each note at the left end of its space.

Ex. 120

All rests (except whole-rests) should be placed on the staff, from left to right, in exactly the same way as notes. Each is placed at the left end of its allotted space.

In a score, notes and rests are placed in vertical alignment according to the beats of the measure.

TWO PARTS ON ONE STAFF

Ex. 121

When two parts are written on one staff, in the score or in the players' parts (as for first and second oboes), certain procedures must be followed to insure clarity.

When the parts are in unison:

(a) one set of notes marked à2 (*à deux*) may be used;

(b) each note-head may have two stems, one up and one down.

When there are two parts differing in pitch but identical in rhythm (c), one stem may be used for both note-heads.

If one part plays while the other rests (d), the stems must make this clear.

Two parts which differ in rhythm (e) must be written with stems going in opposite directions.

Ex. 122

There are at least two times, when two parts are written on one staff, that the parts cannot be in perfect vertical alignment:

(a) When the two parts have notes of different value on the same degree of the staff;

(b) When the two parts have notes on adjoining degrees of the staff

The notes of chords cannot be in perfect alignment if two of the notes are on adjacent degrees of the staff (c). When this occurs, the lower note is placed to the left of the stem, with the higher note on the right.

Ex. 123

Occasionally, when writing two parts on one staff, unisons having different time values occur. The example above shows right and wrong notations.

One note-head can serve for a unison (a) if the meaning is clear and the notation can be read quickly and accurately.

One note-head, for both parts, must *not* be used if:

(b) one part has a white note and the other part has a black note;

(d) one part (only) has a dotted note.

Illustrations (c) and (e) show correct notations.

THREE AND FOUR PARTS ON ONE STAFF

Ex. 124

Sometimes, in a sketch or a condensed score, three or four parts are written on one staff. This should never be done in a full score or in the parts.

When all of the parts have notes of the same values and do not cross (a), there is no problem.

A passage for three horns might be written, in a condensed score or sketch, as shown at (b).

1. The first and second horns are written with stems up.

2. The third horn part is written with stems down.

A similar passage for four horns is shown at (c).

The illustration at (d) shows three parts having notes of different values. A passage of this kind should be written on more than one staff if each part is to be read with accuracy.

The notation shown at (d) is used for piano music since the notes are read and played as chords rather than three separate melodic parts; however, this notation is difficult to read and should be avoided if possible.

LEGER LINES

Ex. 125

Leger (ledger) lines are used to extend the staff above or below. Lege
lines are short lines, but they must be long enough for their ends to show
on either side of a note-head. The lines must be the same distance from the
staff and from each other as the staff lines are from one another.

Notes may be written on the leger lines or in the spaces above and
below them as shown in (a) and (b).

The notes shown at (c) are incorrectly written. The outer line, in each
case, is unnecessary and confusing.

Parts for the first violin, flute, and bass clarinet often contain many note
requiring leger lines. When extracting such parts, it is better to use 10-line
paper, rather than the usual 12-line, so as to have more room between the
staves.

It is well to remember that notes on leger lines take up more room
(horizontally) than similar notes on the staff.

Notes written with leger lines usually have longer stems. These stems
extend to the middle line of the staff.

ALL' OTTAVA

Ex. 126

It is possible to avoid the use of leger lines above the staff (a) by writing
the notes an octave lower than they are to sound and placing the sign *8va - -*
(*all' ottava*) over them (b). This indicates that all of the notes are to be played
an octave higher than they are written. The line of dashes indicates the length
of the passage affected, but the end must be marked plainly with a vertical line

The use of leger lines below the staff (c) may be avoided, in a similar
manner, by writing the notes an octave higher and marking the passage *8va
bassa,* as shown at (d). Such a passage is to be played an octave lower than it
is written.

Pianists find this notation convenient and easy to read.

Players of the orchestral instruments automatically associate fingering
with the written notes, and they prefer to have the passage written with leger
lines.

REHEARSAL NUMBERS

Ex. 127

Rehearsal (location) numbers are essential in all orchestra music. If possible, they should be located at good stopping and starting places in the music. In music of moderate tempo, rehearsal numbers should be placed about every eight measures. Lively $\frac{2}{4}$ or $\frac{6}{8}$ strains may need numbers only every sixteen measures or so.

The rehearsal numbers should be placed above the staff, over a bar-line (when possible), and they should be framed with a circle or a square. (Neat circles can be drawn easily and quickly with a draftsman's bow pen.) When written or framed with colored ink (or pencil) they are more readily located by the players.

When a rehearsal number (or letter) occurs within a rest of two or more measures, the rest must be divided so as to indicate the number of measures before and the number of measures after the rehearsal number. This is illustrated at (b) in the example above.

Rehearsal letters are less satisfactory than rehearsal numbers. Many of the letter names sound quite similar (B,D,E,G) and this is something to be considered in a busy (and somewhat noisy) rehearsal. There are but twenty-six letters; numbers are limitless. This is important in longer compositions.

CUE NOTES

Cue notes are important in all compositions and arrangements for orchestra.

There are two kinds of cues:

1. courtesy cues which help a player to keep his place in the music;
2. substitution cues which are meant to be played under certain conditions.

In printed music, cue notes are small, similar to grace notes. In manuscript, they may be written as small notes, or they may be written in red ink.

When writing cue notes, the rules for the turning of the stems do not apply, except in principle. The stems are placed so that they do not interfere with the notes or rests of the main part. In practice, the stems of cue notes are often turned away from the staff, entirely opposite to the rule for regular notes. Let clarity be the guide.

Rests in the main part are placed differently when cue notes are present. Vertical alignment is not affected, but rests are placed higher or lower on the staff (even above or below the staff) according to the space available. See examples 128, 129, 130, and 132.

Dynamic and expression markings for cues are placed above the stems if the stems go up, or below the stems if the stems go down. See examples 128 and 130(b).

COURTESY CUES

Ex. 128

After a player has had several measures of rest, it helps him to have a few cue notes (for some prominent instrument) before his next entrance. The instrument cued in must be one that he cannot fail to hear (a).

In an extremely long period of rest, a few cue notes placed about midway reassure the player that he is counting correctly. Here, again, the instrument cued in must be one that he is sure to hear (b).

Ex. 129

SERENATA D'AMORE

© 1956 Robbins Music Corp.

If a melodic line is to pass smoothly from one instrument to another, a few cue notes of the first instrument's part will help the player of the second instrument to enter correctly.

SUBSTITUTION CUES

Ex. 130

BALLET PARISIEN

The second kind of cues serve a double purpose:

1. they help the player keep the place during a period of rest;
2. they are of great value to an orchestra lacking complete instrumentation.

When a composer writes for a professional orchestra, he can be sure that he will have available at least 2 oboes, 2 bassoons, 4 horns, and so forth.

When music is written for performance by school or other non-professional orchestras, the composer cannot be sure of having a complete instrumentation. Any important solo for the oboe, for instance, must be cued in for another somewhat similar instrument which is available at that time. This might be a flute, clarinet, muted trumpet, violin, or viola.

Orchestra players understand that they are to play the cue notes giving another instrument's part only in the absence of that instrument.

Ex. 131

SERENATA D'AMORE

Mantovani

© 1956 Robbins Music Corp.

In general, a set of orchestra parts (for non-professional use) cannot have too many cues. Of course, the notation must always be clear, well spaced, and never crowded. Cues are usually placed in a part when that instrument has a rest of a few measures. An instrument rarely needs its own part and a cued in part, too. When this is necessary, two staves may be used. (Ex. 131).

CUES FOR TRANSPOSING INSTRUMENTS

Ex. 132

a.

PETITE BOURRÉE

Angelo de Prosse
Arr. Merle J. Isaac

© 1941 Carl Fischer Inc.   Used by permission.

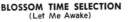

BLOSSOM TIME SELECTION
(Let Me Awake)

Dorothy Donnelly, Sigmund Romberg

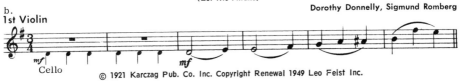

b.

© 1921 Karczag Pub. Co. Inc. Copyright Renewal 1949 Leo Feist Inc.

HÄNSEL AND GRETEL
Selection

E. Humperdinck
Arr. Merle J. Isaac

c.

© 1949 Carl Fischer Inc.   Used by permission.

Cue notes, whether courtesy or substitution, should always be written in the correct clef and key so that the player can read them accurately.

This means that cue notes in a part for a transposing instrument must be transposed exactly the same as the regular notes for the instrument. In example (a) above, the flute part is actually a minor seventh higher than the cue notes indicate. As it is transposed, the clarinet player can easily relate the flute part to his own part and, if necessary, he can play it.

A cello part, in the bass clef, is written in the treble clef when it is cued in a violin part (b).

Similarly, a violin part, when cued in a cello part, is written in the bass clef (c).

MARKS OF EXPRESSION, TEMPO, AND DYNAMICS

The original words given at the beginning of a composition, or section of a composition, to indicate tempo and style (such as Andante, Allegro spiritoso) are always placed *above* the staff with the first letter in vertical alignment with the time-signature. They are set in ordinary type.

In manuscript, these words may be hand lettered or typewritten. They must be neat and legible.

Later modifications of the tempo or style (such as *rit., allarg., dolce, espressivo*) are usually placed *below* the staff, and they are set in italics.

The following words and symbols used to indicate dynamics in music are usually placed *below* the staff.

Ex. 133

cresc.   *molto cresc.*   *dim.*   *decresc.*

ppp   *pp*   *p*   *mp*   *mf*   *f*   *ff*   *fff*

sf   *fz*   *sfz*   *fp*   ⸺

The directions *rit., accel.,* and *a tempo* may be placed either above or below the staff, but below is preferred.

Ex. 134

Whenever possible, marks of expression are placed at the note-head and not at the stem. See the above example (a).

As shown in (c), the marking for detached slurring for string instruments and for soft tonguing for wind instruments (a combination of dots or dashes with slurs) should be written with the dots or dashes next to the note-head and the slurs on the outside.

The passage marked (e) shows exceptions to the rule.

With two parts on one staff (f), the rule is often reversed. The notation must be clear and never crowded.

SLURS

BOURRÉE

G. F. Handel

Slurs are curved lines, somewhat heavy in the middle, tapering to a thin line at either end.

When possible, slurs are placed on the side of the note-heads opposite the stems (a).

Exceptions to this general rule are shown at (b) and (c).

When two parts are written on one staff, the slurs are likely to be over the stems, rather than over the note-heads (d). Example (e) shows the slurs under the stems.

In every case, the slur should be placed so that it will make the notation clear and not crowded.

METRONOME MARKINGS

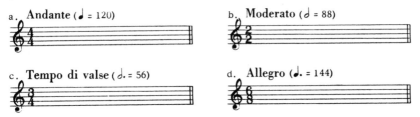

A metronome number is usually added at the beginning of a composition to the word or group of words that indicate general tempo. Formerly, this was written: M.M. ♩ = 120. The initials, M.M., which stand for Maelzel's Metronome, are now omitted.

The note given with the metronome number is usually the same as that indicated by the lower number of the time-signature. Exceptions to this are found in music which is in $\frac{3}{4}$ or $\frac{6}{8}$ time.

Waltzes are often taken "one in a bar" or one beat in a measure. The metronome unit in this case is the dotted half-note (c).

Six-eight time, in fast or moderate tempos, is directed two beats in a measure. The metronome unit with this music is the dotted quarter-note (d). In slow tempos, the eighth-note is the unit.

TRIPLETS

Ex. 137

Occasionally, writers are uncertain about what kinds of notes should be written in triplets. *A triplet is a group of three notes that are played in the time ordinarily given to two such notes.* In the example above, each triplet is equal in time value to the two notes which follow.

Ex. 138

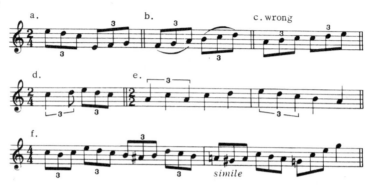

Instrumentalists find it easier to read eighth-note triplets when the numeral 3 is near the beam, not near the note-heads. No slur is needed to indicate that the figure is a triplet (a).

A slur applied to the note-heads indicates that the notes are to be slurred (b). A slur applied to the beam or bracket is vague as to meaning.

The numeral 3 placed near a note-head can be mistaken for a fingering mark (c).

When triplets contain notes not connected with a beam (such as quarter-notes or half-notes), the numeral 3 appears in a bracket (d, e).

If a passage consists largely or entirely of triplets, the numeral 3 may be omitted after the first measure. The word *simile* indicates that the same general effect is to be continued (f).

VARIOUS SIGNS, SYMBOLS, AND WORDS

Many of the directions used in music are placed *over* the staff (except when two parts are written on one staff): muted, open, *pizz., arco, con sordino, senza sordino,* and the signs shown in the example below.

Ex. 139

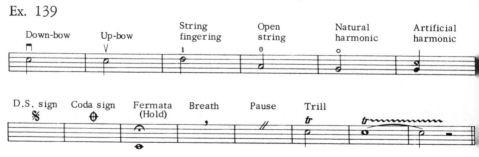

Directions usually placed *below* the staff include the following: *D. S., D. C. al fine,* and *Fine.*

ABBREVIATIONS USED WITH MUSICAL NOTATION

The following example shows time saving abbreviations used in the notation of music. Their use in sketches and full scores is recommended to experienced composers and arrangers. Students will avoid errors by writing out all of the notes, as abbreviations present incomplete pictures.

Abbreviations should seldom be used in orchestra parts. They should never be used unless their meaning is perfectly clear to the reader.

Ex. 140

OUR DIRECTOR

F. E. Bigelow
Arr. Merle J. Isaac

ABBREVIATIONS FOR THE NAMES OF ORCHESTRAL INSTRUMENTS

violin	V., Vn., Vl., Vln.
first violin	V.1, Vn.I, 1st V.
second violin	V.2, Vn.II, 2nd V.
advanced violin	Adv. V.
violins	Vns., Vlns.
viola	Va., Vla.
cello (violoncello)	Cello, Vc.
bass (double bass)	Bass, Db., D.B.
piccolo	Pic., Picc.
flute	Fl.
oboe	Ob.
English horn	Eng. Hn.
clarinet	Cl., Clar.
bass clarinet	Bs. Cl.
bassoon	Bn., Bsn., Bssn.
alto saxophone	A. Sax., Al. Sax., Alto Sax.
tenor saxophone	T. Sax., Tn. Sax., Ten. Sax.
trumpet	Tpt., Trpt.
horn	Hn.
trombone	Tbn., Trb.
tuba	Tuba
snare drum	S.D., Sn.Dr.
bass drum	B.D., Bs.Dr.
timpani	Timp.
cymbal	Cym.
triangle	Tgl., Tri.
tambourine	Tamb.
glockenspiel	Bells
xylophone	Xylo.
piano	Pa.

The expression "first violin" refers to the *part* and means that all of the members of the first violin section play this part.

The expression "violins" refers to more than one violin *part* and would include both the first and the second violin sections.

Similarly, the expression "1st flute" (or Fl. 1) refers to the *part*, not to the *players*. The expression "flutes", then, would refer to both the first and second flute parts.

All plurals are formed by adding the letter "s".

CHAPTER SIX

TRANSPOSITION

Transposition is the changing of music from one key to another. One who writes for orchestral instruments must understand transposition and make use of it constantly. This chapter explains the need for this skill, and gives material for its development.

In Ex. 141 a well-known melody is written in the key of F. Ex. 142 is the same melody transposed one step higher to the key of G.

Ex. 141

Ex. 142

THE TRANSPOSING INSTRUMENTS

In order to explain transposition as it concerns the orchestral instruments, let us suppose that we are present at an orchestra rehearsal. The director has written the note "C" on the blackboard.

Ex. 143

He asks the flute player to play the note as written. Then, going over to the piano, the director strikes C, the note written on the blackboard. He finds that C on the piano has exactly the same pitch as the tone produced by the flute. Musicians say that the flute is a C instrument.

Ex. 144

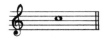

Next, the director asks a clarinetist to play the note that is written on the blackboard. Checking with the piano, the director finds that the tone produced by the clarinetist (called C) is the same pitch as B♭ on the piano. Musicians call the clarinet a B♭ instrument.

Ex. 145

The same procedure is carried out with the trumpet player who produces a tone that he calls C, but which is the same pitch as B♭ on the piano.

Ex. 146

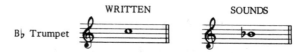

The alto saxophone player reads the written C and sounds a tone that is a major sixth lower: E♭.

A horn player reads the written C, but produces a tone a fifth lower, corresponding to F on the piano.

Ex. 147

The alto saxophone player reads the written C and sounds a tone that is a major sixth lower: E♭.

Ex. 148

The players of the tenor saxophone and the bass clarinet read C, but sound B♭, a major ninth lower.

Ex. 149

Certain other instruments may also be called transposing instruments, because the tones they sound are not the same as the written notes. For example, the orchestra bells sound two octaves higher than the music is written; the piccolo and xylophone sound one octave higher; the string bass sounds an octave lower.

Although the tones sound different from the written notes, the names of the tones are not changed. When the piccolo player reads C, the tone he plays is also named C, though it is an octave higher. Octave transpositions are easy to understand and to use.

Ex. 150

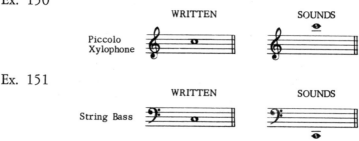

Ex. 151

All of the orchestral instruments in common use which are not discussed in the above paragraphs are non-transposing or C instruments.

WRITING FOR THE TRANSPOSING INSTRUMENTS

In the preceding paragraphs we discussed certain transposing instruments, observing that the players read one note and the instruments sound another. For example, the B♭ clarinet player reads C, but sounds B♭. The tones he plays sound a major second lower than the notes he reads.

This presents a problem, not to the player, but to the arranger. If the instrument *sounds* a major second *lower,* its notes must be *written* a major second *higher* than the tone required. If the clarinet tone is to sound like C on the piano, the arranger must write D in the clarinet part.

Ex. 152 gives part of the song, AMERICA, in the key of F. This melody can be played by the various transposing instruments in the key of F concert (like the key of F sounds on the piano).

Ex. 152

AMERICA

Henry Carey

To play AMERICA in the key of F concert, the B♭ clarinet and the B♭ trumpet must have parts written for them a major second higher, in the key of G, as shown in Ex. 153.

Ex. 153

AMERICA

Henry Carey

The part for the F horn must be written in the key of C, a perfect fifth higher than the concert key.

Ex. 154

AMERICA

Henry Carey

An E♭ alto saxophone must have a part written in the key of D, a major sixth higher than the concert key.

Ex. 155

AMERICA

Henry Carey

The B♭ tenor saxophone and the B♭ bass clarinet must have parts written a major ninth higher, in the key of G.

Ex. 156

AMERICA

Henry Carey

THE TRANSPOSING INSTRUMENTS

Any transposing instrument, when playing the written note "C", will sound the note given in the name of the instrument. The transposition may be a second, a fifth, a sixth, or a ninth, depending upon the instrument, but each instrument will always sound the note for which it is named. The chart below gives the exact transposition for each instrument.

Ex. 157

READING WHAT IS WRITTEN

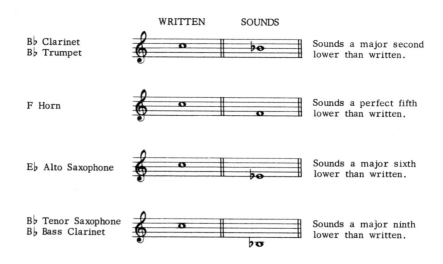

Bb Clarinet
Bb Trumpet — Sounds a major second lower than written.

F Horn — Sounds a perfect fifth lower than written.

Eb Alto Saxophone — Sounds a major sixth lower than written.

Bb Tenor Saxophone
Bb Bass Clarinet — Sounds a major ninth lower than written.

Ex. 158

WRITING WHAT IS WANTED

Bb Clarinet
Bb Trumpet — Write the notes a major second higher than they are to sound.

F Horn — Write the notes a perfect fifth higher than they are to sound.

Eb Alto Saxophone — Write the notes a major sixth higher than they are to sound.

Bb Tenor Saxophone
Bb Bass Clarinet — Write the notes a major ninth higher than they are to sound.

RULES

I. The tones of the B♭ clarinet and the B♭ trumpet sound a major second *lower* than they are written. Write the notes to be played by these instruments a major second *higher* than they are to sound. The key, also, will be a major second higher than the concert key.

II. The tones of the F horn sound a perfect fifth *lower* than they are written. Write the notes to be played by this instrument a perfect fifth *higher* than they are to sound. The key, also, will be a perfect fifth higher than the concert key.

III. The tones of the E♭ alto saxophone sound a major sixth *lower* than they are written. Write the notes to be played by this instrument a major sixth *higher* than they are to sound. The key, also, will be a major sixth higher than the concert key.

IV. The tones of the B♭ bass clarinet and the B♭ tenor saxophone sound a major ninth *lower* than they are written. Write the notes to be played by these instruments a major ninth *higher* than they are to sound. The key will be a major second higher than the concert key.

INTERVALS

To transpose accurately, one must be familiar with the intervals used in the study of harmony. It would be well for the student of orchestration to review these intervals, especially the ones that he finds he needs when writing for transposing instruments.

Ex. 159

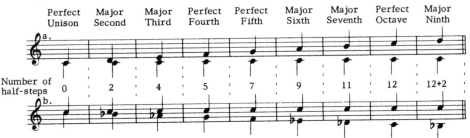

Perfect Unison	Major Second	Major Third	Perfect Fourth	Perfect Fifth	Major Sixth	Major Seventh	Perfect Octave	Major Ninth

Number of half-steps: 0 : 2 : 4 : 5 : 7 : 9 : 11 : 12 : 12+2

Ex. 160

| C | D | E | F | G | A | B | C |

THE PIANO KEYBOARD

EXERCISES WITH INTERVALS

The form below gives the names of seven notes, each at the head of a column. In the spaces below each given note, write the names of the notes requested.

For example, the first given note is C. Line 1 asks for the name of the note that is a major second higher than C. The answer is D. In line 2, give the name of the note that is a major second lower than C. The answer is B♭.

Work out the exercises away from the piano, but be sure to check your answers on a piano keyboard.

Given Notes:	C	A	F♯	D	E♭	B♭	G
1. A major second higher	D						
2. A major second lower	B♭						
3. A perfect fifth higher							
4. A perfect fifth lower							
5. A major sixth higher							
6. A major sixth lower							
7. A major ninth higher							
8. A major ninth lower							

EXERCISES IN TRANSPOSITION

1. Write AMERICA, so that it will sound in the key of E♭ concert, for the following instruments:
   a. B♭ clarinet
   b. F horn
   c. E♭ alto saxophone
   d. B♭ bass clarinet
2. Write SILENT NIGHT, so that it will sound in the key of C concert, for the following instruments:
   a. B♭ trumpet
   b. E♭ alto saxophone
   c. B♭ tenor saxophone
3. For each of the instruments listed below, indicate the key in which a melody would be written so as to have it sound in the given concert key. For example, to have the B♭ clarinet play a melody that sounds in the key of C concert, the part must be written in the key of D. The part for the F horn would need to be written in the key of G.

Concert Keys	C	F	B♭	E♭	G	D
B♭ clarinet	D					
B♭ trumpet						
F horn	G					
E♭ alto saxophone						
B♭ bass clarinet						
B♭ tenor saxophone						

CHAPTER SEVEN

STRING BOWINGS

The term "bowing", as used in orchestra arranging, refers to the various signs and markings given in the string player's parts, indicating the up-bows and down-bows, the legatos and staccatos. Good bowing produces good rhythm. In fact, bowing is the principal means of bringing out not only the rhythm, but also the dynamics, style, and expression.

Bowing is not something that each player can decide for himself during a rehearsal. The music must be marked carefully so that all of the players in a section will give the notes the same interpretation, and so that the various string sections will be in agreement. Generally speaking, an orchestra sounds better and looks better when all of the string instruments are bowed alike most of the time.

The arranger who does not play a string instrument well will need to seek advice from string players or, better still, from string teachers.

The sign ⊓ placed over a note indicates that the note is to be played with a down-bow: the bow moving from the frog toward the point (or tip).

The sign V placed over a note indicates that it is to be played with an up-bow: the bow moving from the point toward the frog.

Whenever possible, the down-bow is used for accented or louder tones; the up-bow for unaccented or softer tones. There are many exceptions, of course, but much of the time the note on the first beat of the measure is played with a down-bow, while the note on the last beat of the measure is played with an up-bow.

When a string passage is written without markings of any kind, the player understands that he is to change the direction of the bow for each successive note and play down-bows and up-bows alternately.

Ex. 161

The use of separate bows, as illustrated above, does not necessarily mean that the tones are to be separated. They are very likely to be played that way, however, unless some direction is given, such as "smoothly" or *sostenuto.*

Separate bows can be played at any tempo and at any dynamic level.

Long, vigorous strokes of the bow at a fast or moderate tempo will produce tones of considerable volume.

Short, light strokes of the bow will produce soft music.

The signs for down-bow and up-bow are needed only at the beginning of a passage, or at some place in the music where the player might be uncertain as to which one to use.

The next type of bowing to be considered is slurring. In string music, the slur does not indicate phrases, as it often does in piano music. It shows which notes are to be played together with one continuous stroke of the bow. The number of notes that can be played in one bow-stroke depends on tempo and dynamics (and the skill of the player).

Ex. 162 illustrates slurring two notes to the bow, with two bows in a measure. At fast or moderate speeds, the player can get considerable volume.

Ex. 162

With four notes to the bow and one bow in a measure there is more smoothness, but less volume.

Ex. 163

Eight notes to the bow, with the bow moving slowly through two measures, will produce a perfect *legato,* but very little volume.

Ex. 164

If the bow moves at the same rate of speed for each slur, the number of notes played in each stroke of the bow will not change the volume. In the following example there are two bow strokes in each measure. Although there are two, four, and eight notes to the bow, all will be equally loud (other things being equal), since in each case the bow is moving at the same speed.

The speed of the bow, not the speed of the notes, determines the volume.

Ex. 165

EXAMPLES OF STRING BOWINGS

SEPARATE BOWS

The following examples give various types of bowings that will be found in music suitable for performance by school orchestras. There are, of course, many more types of string bowings which are suitable for use by advanced players and soloists.

Examples 166 and 167 illustrate separate bows. Notice that the first note in most measures is played with a down-bow. (You might mark them lightly with pencil.) String players prefer to have a down-bow on the accented part of the measure, usually the first beat.

Ex. 166

AWAKE, MY HEART, AND SING
(Choral)

J. Krueger
Arr. Merle J. Isaac

© 1939 Carl Fischer Inc.   Used by permission.

Ex. 167

OYE NEGRA
(Guaracha)

Noro Morales

© 1942 Robbins Music Corp.

SLURS

Examples 168 and 169 illustrate the use of slurs.

The waltz, in $\frac{3}{4}$ time, shows how the down-bows naturally fall on the first beat of each alternate measure.

Ex. 168

WHEN I GROW TOO OLD TO DREAM

Oscar Hammerstein II, Sigmund Romberg

© 1934, 1935 (Renewal 1962, 1963) Metro-Goldwyn-Mayer Inc.

Ex. 169 shows seven and eight short notes in each slur. The music is marked *piano,* and is to be played softly.

Ex. 169

OVER THE RAINBOW

E. Y. Harburg, Harold Arlen

© 1939 Leo Feist Inc.

Ex. 170 is a rather unusual melody, with accents falling on beats other than the first beat of the measure. Notice that, in most instances, the accented notes are played with down-bows.

Ex. 170

SONG OF THE BAYOU

Rube Bloom

© 1929 (Renewal 1957) Leo Feist Inc.

PICK-UP NOTES

Some melodies start on the first beat of the measure, but others start on some beat other than the first. These opening notes, preceding the first full measure, are called pick-up notes. They are customarily bowed so that the first beat of the first full measure will be played with a down-bow.

When there is just one pick-up note, it is usually played with an up-bow.

Ex. 171

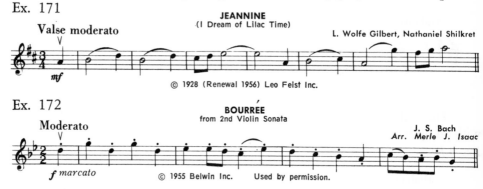

JEANNINE
(I Dream of Lilac Time)

L. Wolfe Gilbert, Nathaniel Shilkret

© 1928 (Renewal 1956) Leo Feist Inc.

Ex. 172

BOURREE
from 2nd Violin Sonata

J. S. Bach
Arr. Merle J. Isaac

© 1955 Belwin Inc.   Used by permission.

Two pick-up notes that are slurred are treated as a single note and are played with an up-bow.

Ex. 173

MINUET
from the "London Symphony"

J. Haydn
Arr. Merle J. Isaac

© 1941 Carl Fischer Inc.   Used by permission.

Ex. 174

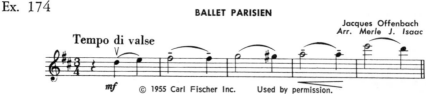

BALLET PARISIEN

Jacques Offenbach
Arr. Merle J. Isaac

© 1955 Carl Fischer Inc.   Used by permission.

Two pick-up notes, of equal value and not slurred, usually start with a down-bow.

Ex. 175

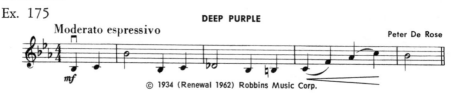

DEEP PURPLE

Peter De Rose

© 1934 (Renewal 1962) Robbins Music Corp.

Ex. 176

Three pick-up notes, of equal value and not slurred, start with an up-bow.

Ex. 177

Ex. 178

Three slurred pick-up notes are treated as a one note pick-up and played with an up-bow.

Ex. 179

Separate Bows and Slurs

Although string passages may be found that are played entirely with separate bows or entirely with slurs, most music for strings makes use of both separate bows and slurs. This combination is most effective and provides excellent contrast and variety.

Ex. 180

Ex. 181

DETACHED SLURS

A type of orchestral bowing that is very useful, and in some rhythm patterns indispensable, is shown in the next group of examples. It has several names, but can be called a "detached slur" since the tones are detached and the bow travels in the same direction for both. The bow stops, however, during the slur, and there is a definite separation between the tones. The detached slur is somewhat easier and more natural to play on an up-bow. In a series of detached slurs, however, alternating down-bows and up-bows may be used freely.

Ex. 182

Ex. 183

Ex. 184

Another type of bowing, similar to the detached slur, is indicated with dashes instead of dots. The tones are separated very slightly, almost imperceptibly, while the player gives the bow a series of pressures or pushes, two or three, in the same direction. This bowing is most often used in slow, sustained passages.

Ex. 185

Ex. 186

LIFTING THE BOW

Although bowing, on a string instrument, commonly makes use of alternate down-bows and up-bows, there are times when two or more down-bows or up-bows may be used in succession. The detached slur, for example, is really two down-bows or two up-bows. The bow stops between the tones, remains on the string, and then continues in the same direction.

In other cases, after playing one stroke, the bow is lifted off the string and then replaced, near the frog or the point, ready for the next stroke. This type of bowing occurs most frequently with successive down-bows.

Ex. 187

ALLA TURCA

E. Schmidt, Op. 19, No. 8
Arr. Merle J. Isaac

© 1941 Carl Fischer Inc.   Used by permission.

Chords are usually played with down-bows. In a series of two or more chords it is, of course, necessary to lift the bow between the strokes.

Ex. 188

MANITOU
Indian Dance

Courtney Drake
Arr. Merle J. Isaac

© 1938 Carl Fischer Inc.   Used by permission.

CERTAIN TRIPLETS

A triplet on an unaccented beat, followed by a note on an accented beat, will usually start with an up-bow.

Ex. 189

RENDEZVOUS

W. Aletter
Arr. Merle J. Isaac

© 1955 Belwin Inc.   Used by permission.

Ex. 190

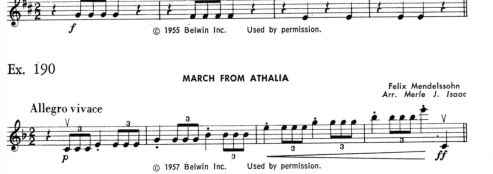

MARCH FROM ATHALIA

Felix Mendelssohn
Arr. Merle J. Isaac

© 1957 Belwin Inc.   Used by permission.

TREMOLO

Tremolo bowing corresponds to the roll on the drum. It is a continuous series of short tones repeated as rapidly as possible. It is equally effective loud or soft and, like drum rolls, makes excellent *crescendos* and *diminuendos*. Usually a tremolo passage has relatively few changes of pitch.

Ex. 191

RUSSIAN SAILORS' DANCE
from "The Red Poppy"

Reinhold Gliere
Arr. Merle J. Isaac

Prestissimo

© 1940 Carl Fischer Inc.   Used by permission.

Ex. 192

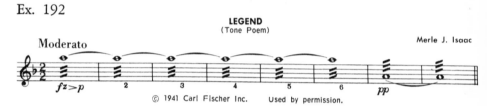

LEGEND
(Tone Poem)

Merle J. Isaac

Moderato

© 1941 Carl Fischer Inc.   Used by permission.

PERPETUAL MOTION BOWING

Another easy and effective type of bowing, similar to tremolo, consists of a continuous series of sixteenth-notes with two or more tones having the same pitch. It is equally effective loud or soft. Some writers call this bowing "measured tremolo". However, since it is rhythmic, it is not a true tremolo.

Ex. 193

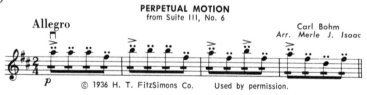

PERPETUAL MOTION
from Suite III, No. 6

Carl Bohm
Arr. Merle J. Isaac

Allegro

© 1936 H. T. FitzSimons Co.   Used by permission.

Ex. 194

CAVALIER OVERTURE

Merle J. Isaac

Grandioso

© 1940 Carl Fischer Inc.   Used by permission.

ACCOMPANIMENT PARTS

Accompaniment parts present certain rhythmic patterns which are less common in melody parts. In a melody, accented beats are played with down-bows and unaccented beats with up-bows. In an accompaniment passage consisting of afterbeats, however, there are no notes on accented beats, but only rests. In this case, the stronger afterbeat in the measure will be played with a down-bow and the weaker will be taken up-bow.

Ex. 195

PIZZICATO PLAYING

Pizzicato playing is not actually a bowing problem, since the bow is not used while the strings are being plucked by the fingers. When a pizzicato passage is but a small part of a composition, the players keep their bows in their hands. However, if the composition is to be played pizzicato throughout, the players may place their bows on the music stands.

Following are a few pizzicato problems that the arranger must consider.

While all of the tones, high or low, that can be played with the bow can also be played pizzicato, some tones are less satisfactory.

The extremely high tones on each instrument are not generally effective. The lowest string on the string bass should be avoided.

Ex. 196

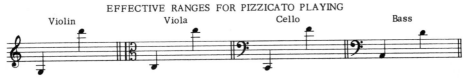

EFFECTIVE RANGES FOR PIZZICATO PLAYING

The players need a little time to change from pizzicato playing to arco playing (with the bow). In the following examples, notice that there is a rest preceding each change.

Ex. 197

JEANNINE
(I Dream of Lilac Time)

L. Wolfe Gilbert, Nathaniel Shilkret

Valse moderato

© 1928 (Renewal 1956) Leo Feist Inc.

Ex. 198

HOPAK
from "The Fair at Sorochinsk"

M. Moussorgsky
Arr. Merle J. Isaac

© 1957 Belwin Inc.   Used by permission.

Notation is somewhat different when music is written for pizzicato playing. Half-notes are not used, nor, as a rule, are eighth-notes followed by eighth-rests. No slurs, of course, nor dots or dashes. An occasional accent mark is useful.

Ex. 199

INCORRECT NOTATION   CORRECT NOTATION

Tones that are played pizzicato need not be loud to be heard. They carry well, especially those played by the string bass.

Pizzicato passages should rarely be marked *ff*. If the player tries to play loudly, he will get more noise than musical tone.

While a few tones played *pp* are effective as contrast, *p*, *mf*, and *f* are the safest dynamic levels to use.

Moderation in tempo, too, is generally most effective for pizzicato playing. Since the tones are of such short duration, slow playing may sound empty. Rapid playing, however, may become quite difficult, especially if continuous.

A series of eighth-notes is much more difficult and tiring than a passage containing both eighth-notes and quarter-notes.

In the following example, notice how the effect of continuous eighth-notes is obtained by alternating the eighth-notes in the first and second violin parts.

Ex. 200

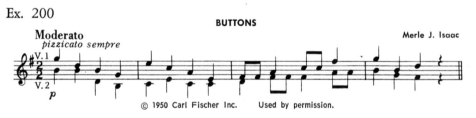

BUTTONS

Moderato
pizzicato sempre

Merle J. Isaac

© 1950 Carl Fischer Inc.   Used by permission.

MUTES

Mutes, for string instruments, look something like combs having only three teeth. They are made of wood, plastic, or other material, and fit on the bridge, over the strings.

Mutes affect the tone of the instruments, reducing the volume and changing the tone color. Strings can play softly without mutes, but their use gives the tone a unique quality: veiled and mysterious.

Players need a little time (a couple of measures) for putting on or taking off mutes. The usual directions are *con sordini* (with mutes) and *senza sordini* (without mutes).

SUMMARY

To an experienced string player, a passage feels right, as to bowing, if it has the following characteristics:

1. The first note in most measures is played with a down-bow. (Ex. 166). In waltz time, the down-bows are likely to occur on the first beat of every alternate measure (Ex. 168).

2. Accented notes are played with down-bows (Ex. 170).

3. Pick-up notes are bowed so that the first beat of the first full measure is played with a down-bow (Ex. 171).

    a. A single pick-up note, or a slurred group, is played with an up-bow (Ex. 172, 174).

    b. The first of two pick-up notes, not slurred, is played with a down-bow (Ex. 175).

    c. The first of three pick-up notes, or three slurred groups, is played with an up-bow (Ex. 177, 178, 179).

4. The following time-figures are bowed as indicated:

Ex. 201

5. Chords are played with down-bows (Ex. 188).

6. A triplet on an unaccented beat starts with an up-bow (Ex. 189).

7. The player never feels that too many notes are slurred together, and that he is going to run out of bow.

8. Time is given for changing from *pizzicato* to *arco* or the reverse.

9. Time is given for putting on a mute or removing one.

10. The last note of the composition is played with a down-bow (unless it is marked *crescendo*).

CHAPTER EIGHT

WIND ARTICULATIONS

The term "articulation", as it is used by musicians, has more than one meaning. To some, articulation refers to the manner in which a tone is started on a wind instrument. In this sense, the word "tonguing" can generally be used. As it will be used in this chapter, the word articulation will include not only tonguing, but also all of the various ways that tones can be put together in sequence. This includes the many degrees and combinations of legatos and staccatos.

Musicians, unfortunately, do not agree on the exact meanings of the various signs that are used to indicate articulations. A dot or a dash may mean one thing to a pianist, another thing to a string player, and something still different to a wind player. Worse than this, the wind players do not agree among themselves.

Orchestras will produce better sounding music when all concerned — composers, conductors, and performers — agree on the articulations to be used in passages played by the wind instruments. To convey this information in writing, we must have symbols that mean the same to all persons concerned. These do not exist at the present time, but we must work toward that goal.

There are but two fundamental articulations: slurring and tonguing. These are used in various combinations.

SLURS

A slur is a curved line over or under two or more notes, indicating that only the first note is to be tongued. The other tones follow without separation or interruption of any kind. As will be seen in the following examples, slurs can be very short or very long.

Ex. 202

MISSISSIPPI SUITE
(Old Creole Days)

© 1926 (Renewal 1954) Leo Feist Inc.

Ex. 203

RUMANIAN OVERTURE

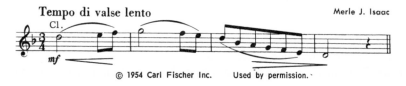

© 1954 Carl Fischer Inc.   Used by permission.

Ex. 204

LOHENGRIN
From the Opera

Richard Wagner

When tones are slurred on a wind instrument, the first tone is tongued, and the others follow without any separations between them. There is little difference of opinion as to how this should be done, though the first tone can be tongued gently (using the syllable "doo") or it can be tongued forcibly (using the syllable "too").

On the other hand, when all of the tones are tongued, all of the tones are separated. They may be separated ever so little or ever so much. This permits different interpretations and raises the question: when tones are to be separated, how much are they to be separated?

The words *legato* and *staccato* are avoided by many musicians because, through the years, misconceptions have arisen concerning their meanings. These two words, however, are really quite useful if we accept them as meaning "tones connected" and "tones separated" — just that and no more.

In a truly *legato* passage, all of the tones are connected (though not necessarily slurred), and the tones receive all, or very nearly all, of the time values which the notes indicate.

In a *staccato* passage, all of the tones are shortened, in varying degrees, and they are separated from one another. Staccato tones do not receive the full time values indicated by the notes. It should be noted, however, that the length of a staccato tone added to the length of the separation equals the full value of the note.

STACCATO

Ordinary *staccato* is indicated in music by placing a dot above or below a note (opposite the stem). The dot indicates that the note is to receive approximately half its value. In a series of staccato tones there will be rests (periods of silence) following the tones equal in length to the shortened tones themselves.

Ex. 205

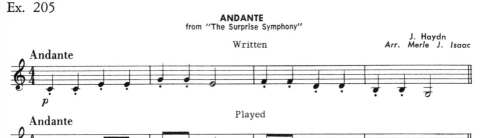

ANDANTE
from "The Surprise Symphony"

Written

J. Haydn
Arr. Merle J. Isaac

Played

© 1941 Carl Fischer Inc.   Used by permission.

In the above example, it will be seen that music written with quarter-notes and dots is much easier to read than music written with eighth-notes and eighth-rests. The music, however, could have been written and read either way.

In the next example, the use of the dots greatly simplifies the notation. Rests of the correct value placed between all of the notes in this passage would be difficult to write and difficult to read.

Ex. 206

MISSISSIPPI SUITE
(Mardi Gras)

Allegro

Cl.

Ferde Grofe

STACCATISSIMO

A small, vertical wedge over or under a note (opposite the stem) indicates a sharp staccato, sometimes called *staccatissimo.* When notes are marked in this manner, each tone is produced by a forceful attack of the tongue, and is shortened to about one-fourth of its written value. These tones are likely to be played *forte.*

Ex. 207

LEGEND OF TSAR SALTAN

Allegro

Ob. & Cl.

N. Rimsky-Korsakov

ACCENTS

An accent mark ($>$) placed over or under a note usually indicates that the tone is to be tongued with definite stress and emphasis. In some cases, the loudness of the tone diminishes quickly after the forceful attack.

Ex. 208

SYMPHONY No. 5
"From the New World"

Allegro con fuoco

Fl.

Antonin Dvorak

Ex. 209

SYMPHONY No. 8
(The "Unfinished")

Andante con moto

Fl.

Franz Schubert

In other cases, the volume of the accented tone remains constant.

Ex. 210

LES PRÉLUDES

Andante maestoso

Tpt.

Franz Liszt

Accented tones are usually tongued, but this is not always so. The following example illustrates accented tones within a group of slurred tones. The player stresses or emphasizes these accented tones by making them louder than the adjoining tones.

Ex. 211

When accented tones occur in a series, they are usually separated. This is particularly true if the music is loud or rhythmic, maestoso or marcato.

Ex. 212

Ex. 213

TENUTO

A short, horizontal line placed above or below a note indicates that the note is to receive nearly its full value. Some writers call this mark *tenuto*. It usually indicates that the tone is to be tongued neither lightly nor forcibly, but just in the ordinary manner. The tones are to be given almost their full value, but are shortened just enough to prevent their being connected.

Ex. 214

Ex. 215

LEGATO TONGUING

When the player of a wind instrument starts a tone, he usually tongues it. First, he holds his tongue in such a way that it stops his breath from entering the instrument. Then, he pulls back his tongue (as in saying *too* or *doo*), and the air, which is under pressure from the diaphragm, rushes into the mouthpiece or reed. The force of this rush of air starts the vibration of the air column within the instrument.

This valve-like action of the tongue in starting a tone is known as an attack. Actually, so far as the air is concerned, it is more of a release. The tone is attacked when the air is released.

Accented tones are usually tongued forcibly, using the syllable *too* with considerable air pressure.

Another style of playing is known as legato tonguing or soft tonguing. The tones are tongued gently, using the syllable *doo*. Usually the air pressure is low and the tones are not loud. Legato tonguing is indicated with a slur and either dots or dashes. The tones are played in a connected manner, as though they were slurred, but each tone is tongued very gently and there is a slight interruption between the tones.

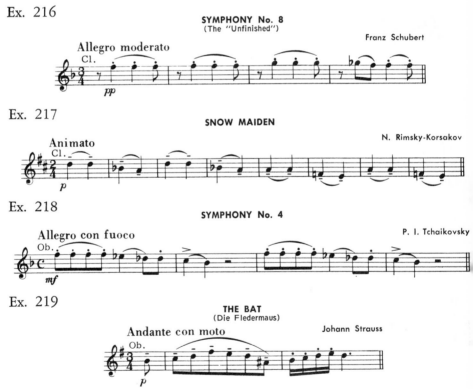

Ex. 216

SYMPHONY No. 8
(The "Unfinished")

Franz Schubert

Ex. 217

SNOW MAIDEN

N. Rimsky-Korsakov

Ex. 218

SYMPHONY No. 4

P. I. Tchaikovsky

Ex. 219

THE BAT
(Die Fledermaus)

Johann Strauss

The above examples, written with dots and slurs and with dashes and slurs, are played in much the same way. Musicians would do well to clarify markings such as these, because finer distinctions in meaning would produce better interpretations. In the meantime, dots will probably suggest shorter tones and dashes longer tones. The slur indicates that all tones are to be played with soft tonguing and that the separations are to be slight.

STACCATO TONES FOLLOWING SLURS

The examples given below show woodwind passages consisting of alterating groups of slurred notes and staccato notes. All are excerpts from rhythnic passages played at a fairly rapid tempo.

Letter (a), in each example, shows the passage as it would ordinarily be written. Letter (b) shows a better notation. Experienced musicians would read the notes given at letter (a) and play them as given at letter (b). School musicians, however, need the help provided by the more accurate notation.

Students will observe that, in the recommended notation, accents have been added to notes on the first beat of the measure and slurs have been extended. The most important difference, however, may be stated as a basic principle: Shorten the last slurred note preceding a staccato note.

Ex. 222 illustrates a similar problem in the notation of articulation.

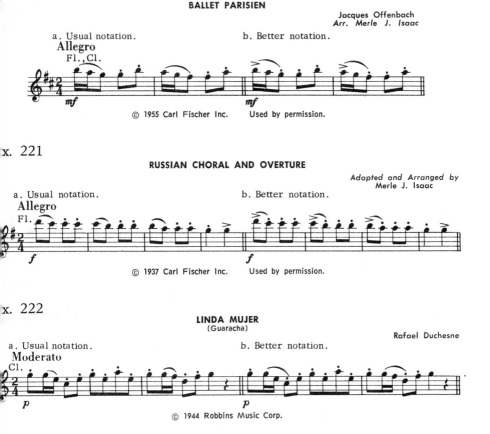

Ex. 220

BALLET PARISIEN

Jacques Offenbach
Arr. Merle J. Isaac

a. Usual notation.

b. Better notation.

Allegro
Fl., Cl.

© 1955 Carl Fischer Inc.   Used by permission.

Ex. 221

RUSSIAN CHORAL AND OVERTURE

Adapted and Arranged by
Merle J. Isaac

a. Usual notation.

b. Better notation.

Allegro
Fl.

© 1937 Carl Fischer Inc.   Used by permission.

Ex. 222

LINDA MUJER
(Guaracha)

Rafael Duchesne

a. Usual notation.

b. Better notation.

Moderato
Cl.

© 1944 Robbins Music Corp.

DOUBLE AND TRIPLE TONGUING

A player on a wind instrument ordinarily starts a tone by tonguing it, using the syllable *too* or *doo*. In a rapid passage, the player may use the syllables *too* and *koo* alternately. This is known as double tonguing. It may be notated as shown in Ex. 223.

Ex. 223

SCHEHERAZADE

N. Rimsky-Korsako

Triple tonguing is a very rapid form of articulation. The player uses th syllables *ta-ta-ka* or *ta-ka-ta*. (Ex. 224).

Ex. 224

SCHEHERAZADE

N. Rimsky-Korsako

Double and triple tonguing are most effective on the flute and trumpe They are not very practical on the other woodwind instruments, and they a less effective on the lower brass instruments. These special effects should n be used in easy school music.

FORZANDO, SFORZANDO, AND FORTE-PIANO

While not really articulations, there are a few special effects that win instruments can perform very effectively. Examples follow:

Ex. 225

SYMPHONY No. 5

Ludwig van Beethoven

Ex. 226

SYMPHONY No. 5
"From the New World"

Antonin Dvorak

In the above examples, certain notes are marked to indicate that they a to be emphasized and played louder than the surrounding notes. In most cas the tone is to be started loud, then the volume is to be reduced quickly.

The following terms and their abbreviations are used to indicate accents of this kind.

forzando	*fz*
forzato	*fz*
sforzando	*sf, sfz*
sforzato	*sf, sfz*
forte-piano	*fp*

The *sforzando* and similar accents may be applied to music at any dynamic level. While these accents are more often found in loud passages, they may also be used effectively in soft passages. The accent indicates emphasis and contrast, rather than volume.

At this point, the student must be reminded again that composers, conductors, and performers are not in agreement as to the exact meanings of the various signs and symbols used to indicate articulations and similar effects on the wind instruments.

The composer or arranger who wishes to have his music played in a specific manner should make use of multiple directions. When a note is marked *sf* or *fz,* without a *decrescendo* sign (⊒>), the tone is likely to be played loud and long. If the composer wishes the volume to diminish or the tones to be separated, he must be specific in his markings.

Study the examples shown in this chapter, and see how the composers have meticulously marked articulations.

STRING BOWINGS AND WIND ARTICULATIONS

Generally speaking, a melodic line played in unison or in octaves by a string instrument and a wind instrument should be similar in every way. A slur in one part, for example, would indicate the use of a slur in the other. This is especially true in easy music where simplicity, rather than complexity, is desired.

The important thing, however, is the way the music sounds, rather than the way it looks. In Ex. 227, the detached slurs in the violin part and the legato tonguing in the trumpet part will produce similar articulations: the tones will be legato, with slight interruptions.

In measures 5 through 8, the trumpet can easily play the four measure slur (with legato tonguing), but the violins can slur only one measure effectively. Both instruments will produce a smooth, legato phrase if well played.

Ex. 228 shows a passage in which the clarinet can slur nine notes effectively, but the violins play only four notes in a bow. In part, this is to make the bowing come out right in the measure which follows.

Ex. 229 illustrates the fact that separate bows on a string instrument can be played very rapidly, producing considerable volume. On a wind instrument it is difficult to tongue all of the tones in a rapid passage and, when so tongued, the volume is reduced. On a wind instrument, slurs are best for fast, loud passages of this kind.

In Ex. 230, the flute articulations and the violin bowing will sound very much the same. Later, in this composition, the flute part is marked like the violin part.

118

Ex. 227

YOU WERE MEANT FOR ME

Arthur Freed, Nacio Herb Brown

Ex. 228

SONG OF THE BAYOU

Rube Bloom

Ex. 229

SYMPHONY No. 4

P. I. Tchaikovsky

Ex. 230

THE NUTCRACKER SUITE

P. I. Tchaikovsky

SUMMARY

1. The symbols used to indicate articulations on the wind instruments, and even the word articulation itself, do not mean the same things to all persons.

2. Articulation, in this book, refers to the way that tones produced on wind instruments are fitted together in sequence. It includes tonguing and the many kinds of legatos and staccatos.

3. In a slur, only the first tone is tongued (gently, moderately, or forcibly), and the other tones follow without interruption.

4. *Legato* means "tones connected" and *staccato* means "tones separated".

5. In ordinary *staccato,* indicated by a dot, a tone receives about half the value of the note.

6. In *staccatissimo,* indicated by a vertical wedge, a tone receives about one-fourth the value of the note.

7. An accent mark usually indicates that the tone is to be tongued forcibly and that the tone is to be louder than the adjoining tones. Accented tones in a series are usually separated.

8. A short, horizontal line *(tenuto)* indicates that the tone is to receive nearly the full value of the note.

9. In *legato* tonguing, indicated by a slur and dots or dashes, the tones are played in a connected manner much as in a slur. However, each tone is tongued very gently and quickly (with *doo*) and separated ever so slightly.

10. When groups of slurred notes and *staccato* notes occur in sequence, the last slurred note preceding a *staccato* note should be shortened.

11. Double tonguing *(too-koo)* and triple tonguing *(ta-ta-ka* or *ta-ka-ta)* are effective, though not easy, on the flute and the trumpet. They are not practical on the other woodwinds, and are less effective on the lower brass instruments.

12. *Sforzando* accents are very effective with wind instruments. When used, the markings should indicate whether the tones are to be played loud and long, or loud and separated. Accents indicate contrast, rather than volume, and are equally effective in soft passages.

13. The articulations to be used in wind passages should be marked fully and in detail if the composer wishes the part to be played in a specific manner.

14. A melodic line played in unison by a string instrument and a wind instrument should generally be bowed and articulated very much alike. The important thing, however, is the way the music sounds, not the way it looks.

CHAPTER NINE

PART WRITING

WHAT IS A MELODY?

Any succession of single tones may be called a melody. In most melodies, the tones are arranged in a smooth, coherent progression to produce a satisfactory, musical effect.

All melodies are based upon the tones of the scale (and their chromatic alterations) and the tones of the chords built upon the scale. (The scale itself is a melody.)

A melody may follow the tones of the scale upward or downward in whole-step and half-step progressions. Or, a melody may skip from one chord tone to another (as a bugle call). Melodies, therefore, consist of steps and skips.

Good melodies are usually singable. Diatonic steps and half-steps are easy to sing. Some skips are easy (third, fifth, octave), while others are difficult (major seventh, augmented fourth). Singable melodies contain no awkward intervals or passages that sound as if they contained wrong notes.

A good melody has unity and variety. It has a climax and a cadence.

MELODIES ARE CLASSIFIED FOR STUDY

One who writes melodies should study the construction of many successful melodies as well as books on melody writing and counterpoint. Great melodies are not written because composers read books of rules, but those who propose to write melodies should study a few guiding principles and then use or not use them as they think best.

Melodies may be classified in many ways. For our purposes in this chapter, melodies will be classified as follows:

    A. Principal Melodies
    B. Secondary Melodies
        1. Bass Parts
        2. Inside Parts
        3. Accompaniment Parts
        4. Counter-Melodies
        5. Figuration

PRINCIPAL MELODIES

The principal melody of a musical composition is the melody that is most obvious, the one that is most readily heard. It is the melody that we sing or whistle, the one we use to identify the music. When people refer to the melody of a composition, they mean the principal melody.

The principal melody is the only one that can stand independently.

A short composition may contain just one principal melody. Longer compositions contain several principal melodies, heard in succession.

Ex. 231

Ex. 231 gives excerpts from well-known principal melodies.

(a) (b) The simplest melody consists of repetition of the same tone.

(c) (d) Some melodies consist almost entirely of steps.

(e) (f) Less frequently, melodies consist largely of skips.

In general, the melodies that we all know and like consist of both steps and skips, with more steps than skips.

This principle applies to secondary melodies also.

SECONDARY MELODIES

While principal melodies are the ones we notice and remember, all or chestra arrangements contain several secondary melodies which are played a the same time as the principal melodies. Because these melodies are less con spicuous, we are less likely to notice and remember them.

To be well written, however, each of these secondary melodies must be fairly melodious, within the requirements and the limitations of the part.

The various secondary melodies are also known as subordinate parts. To be discussed first are the Bass Parts.

Ex. 232

BASS PARTS

Ex. 232 illustrates various bass melodies that may be used with a given harmony.

(a) The bass part contains only the roots of the tonic and dominant chords. This kind of a bass part is almost adequate for simple folk dances, but it is monotonous and uninteresting.

(b) Here, the root of each chord alternates with the fifth of the chord.

(c) Root, third, fifth, and seventh are all used.

(d)(e) These are other arrangements, using the various chord tones with brief scalewise passages.

(f) This is a more prominent bass part, using many passing tones.

One cannot write a bass part without knowing the principal melody. The bass part (d), which has an E in the second measure, would not be satisfactory if the principal melody also consisted of E in the same measure. Except when it is the root of the chord, the bass note should rarely be the same as the melody note.

Ex. 233

CHARACTERISTIC BASS PARTS

MARCHING ALONG TOGETHER

Edward Pola, Franz Steininger

a. **Tempo di marcia**

LINDA MUJER
(Guaracha)

Rafael Duchesne

b. **Moderato**

I'M AN OLD COWHAND

Johnny Mercer

c. **Brightly**

HYMNUS

A. von Fielitz
Arr. Merle J. Isaac

d. **Andante religioso**

Ex. 233 shows instrumental bass parts of different styles.

(a) A bass part for a simple march may be largely of the "do-so" type. An occasional scalewise passage makes it more interesting.

(b) Some kinds of dance music require rhythmic bass parts. The one shown here is not melodic, in the usual sense, but it sounds quite effective.

(c) Some bass parts include extended scalewise passages.

(d) A bass part for a chorale may have about the same style and rhythm as the principal melody and may make a duet with it.

Bass parts, in instrumental music, usually contain more skips than steps, but a bass part should seldom be all skips. The use of steps increases the melodic quality of the part.

INSIDE PARTS

Most orchestral numbers have good principal melodies and fairly good bass parts. Too frequently the inside parts are uninteresting and unmusical: for instance, the part for the first violin usually is tuneful, but the parts for the second violin and the viola are barren of melodic interest. This does not mean that an alto part should be as florid and brilliant as a soprano part. It should not be.

Inside parts must *support* the principal melody, not detract from it. They must be less active than the outside parts. The less prominent the part, the more simple it should be.

Inside parts usually consist of steps and small skips. While a principal melody may contain a few difficult intervals and still be singable, an inside part with the same difficult intervals would be questionable.

Many limitations are placed upon the arranger. The principal melody cannot be changed. The bass and the harmony may be changed very little. The inside parts must harmonize with the principal melody, with the bass part, and with each other. They must be suited to the instruments for which they are written and to the ability of the performers.

With these principles in mind, the arranger must use his skill and ingenuity to write inside parts that are interesting and attractive.

Ex. 234

a.

Moderato — 1st Violin — YOU WERE MEANT FOR ME — Arthur Freed, Nacio Herb Brown

b.

Tempo di valse — 1st Violin — HI-LILI, HI-LO — Helen Deutsch, Bronislau Kaper

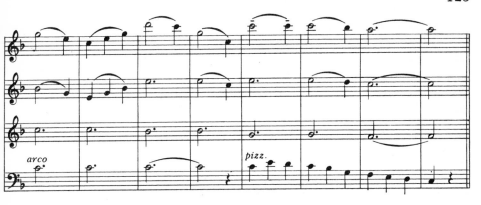

I'M IN THE MOOD FOR LOVE

Jimmy McHugh, Dorothy Fields

c. **Slowly**

© 1935 (Renewal 1963) Robbins Music Corp.

Ex. 234 contains excerpts of string parts from arrangements of popular songs. Play each part alone, on the instrument for which it is written or on the piano.

Then play the parts in combinations. Pay attention to their strengths and weaknesses. Notice, especially, that there are times when the harmony is incomplete or when one tone in a chord is doubled (contrary to the rules of four-part harmony).

Good melody in the parts is more important than complete harmony. The horizontal aspects of the music (counterpoint) are more important than the vertical aspects (harmony).

The arranger must observe the two aspects very closely and try to write both good counterpoint and good harmony.

The arrangements shown in Ex. 234 were written so that the first and second violin parts sound well together without the viola part. When the viola part is added, the music becomes more interesting and the harmony more complete. This method is highly recommended for school and amateur orchestras whose viola sections may be weak or missing. It is not required when writing for professional orchestras certain to have complete instrumentation.

A fundamental principle of part writing is shown in the first four measures of Ex. 234 (a) YOU WERE MEANT FOR ME. The first violin part has quarter-notes in the first and third measures and whole-notes in the second and fourth. The viola part is just the opposite: when the first violin has a whole-note, the viola has four quarter-notes.

This plan of having several short tones in one part while the other part has a long tone is sometimes thought of as "filling in the holes". The moving voice keeps the rhythm going while the other voice sustains.

ACCOMPANIMENT PARTS

In one sense, all secondary or subordinate parts which serve to accompany a principal melody are accompaniment parts. However, as commonly used, the term refers to parts (usually inside parts) which are rhythmic and harmonic, rather than melodic.

Inside parts support the principal melody by filling out the harmony, and by creating some harmonic rhythm with passing notes, suspensions, and the like. Accompaniment parts support the principal melody also by filling out the harmony, but stress rhythm, rather than melody.

Ex. 235

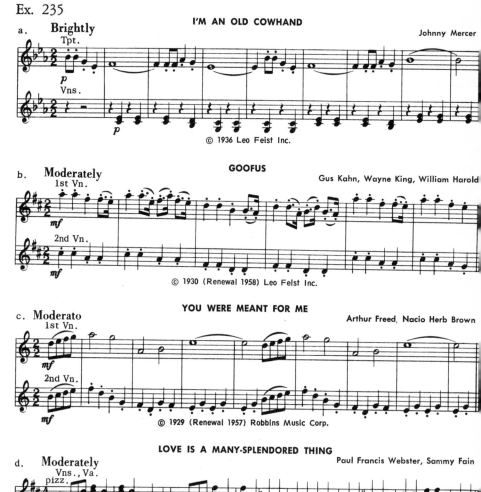

a. **Brightly** I'M AN OLD COWHAND Johnny Mercer

© 1936 Leo Feist Inc.

b. **Moderately** GOOFUS Gus Kahn, Wayne King, William Harold

© 1930 (Renewal 1958) Leo Feist Inc.

c. **Moderato** YOU WERE MEANT FOR ME Arthur Freed, Nacio Herb Brown

© 1929 (Renewal 1957) Robbins Music Corp.

d. **Moderately** LOVE IS A MANY-SPLENDORED THING Paul Francis Webster, Sammy Fain

© 1955 Twentieth Century Music Corp.

Ex. 235 illustrates types of accompaniment parts.

(a) The trumpet plays the melody, while violins play the traditional after-beats. For certain kinds of music, this style of accompaniment sounds satisfactory to the listener, but it is seldom satisfactory to those who play the after-beats. After-beats are not easy to play, and they are not musically satisfying.

(b) Here the after-beats are disguised by adding similar accompaniment tones on the beats. This makes the part much easier to play rhythmically, and gives it a somewhat melodic character.

(c) Here again, the after-beats are actually in the part, but they are played between chord tones on the beat. This part is fairly melodic, and it duets with the principal melody at times.

(d) The violins and violas play harp-like broken chords pizzicato against a smooth cello melody. This is very effective for a limited time, in this case eight measures.

COUNTER-MELODIES

An important part of all arranging is the writing of counter-melodies. A composition may have one counter-melody, or it may have several in succession (as with principal melodies).

The counter-melody is the theme next in line to the principal melody. The audience will hear the counter-melody to a greater extent than they will hear the other secondary parts. While a counter-melody has considerable independence, it cannot stand alone.

A counter-melody must meet many requirements. It must harmonize with the principal melody, with the bass part, and with all other parts.

The music must be arranged so that the counter-melody will be heard. This involves contrast in register, rhythm, and tone color.

The counter-melody must be well suited to the instrument for which it is written and to the ability of the performers.

Ex. 236

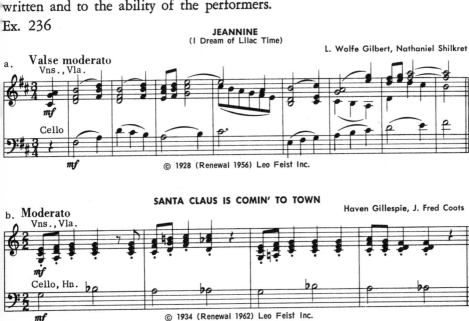

JEANNINE
(I Dream of Lilac Time)

L. Wolfe Gilbert, Nathaniel Shilkret

© 1928 (Renewal 1956) Leo Feist Inc.

SANTA CLAUS IS COMIN' TO TOWN

Haven Gillespie, J. Fred Coots

© 1934 (Renewal 1962) Leo Feist Inc.

128

OVER THE RAINBOW

E. Y. Harburg, Harold Arlen

c. **Moderato**
Obs., Cls.

Hn.

© 1939 Leo Feist Inc.

ANDANTE
from "The Surprise Symphony"

J. Haydn
Arr. Merle J. Isaac

d. **Andante**
Fl., Ob.

Vns.

© 1941 Carl Fischer Inc.   Used by permission.

SOUTH AMERICAN OVERTURE

Merle J. Isaac

e. **Tempo di tango**
Vns.
pizz.

Tpt. muted

© 1951 Carl Fischer Inc.   Used by permission.

MEXICAN OVERTURE

Merle J. Isaac

f. **Moderato**
Vns., W.W.

Cello, Hn.

© 1944 Carl Fischer Inc.   Used by permission.

MISSISSIPPI SUITE
(Mardi Gras)

Ferde Grofe

g. **Maestoso**
Tpts.

Tbns.

© 1926 (Renewal 1954) Leo Feist Inc.

Ex. 236 gives a number of illustrations of characteristic counter-melodies.

(a) Counter-melodies are often given to the cello. The cello register is excellent, being about an octave below the principal melody played by the first violins. In this register, the cello has the tone color needed to bring out its part.

In this excerpt, the rhythm of the counter-melody differs from that of the principal melody. This contrast helps to give the part independence and individuality. Play this counter-melody on the cello and note that it could almost be a principal melody.

(b) This counter-melody is not very melodic, but its sustaining character, contrasting with the light and lively principal melody, makes it most effective. A counter-melody often consists of longer tones than the principal melody which it accompanies.

(c) Although they are melodic and expressive, the fragments given to the horn are not true counter-melodies. They serve to fill in the empty space made in the principal melody by the whole-notes, and they add much to the rhythmic flow.

(d) While most counter-melodies are below the principal melody, this one is above. Played by woodwind instruments in a sustained style, it affords excellent and beautiful contrast to the principal melody played by the strings.

(e) The principal melody in quarter and eighth notes is played pizzicato by the violins while a muted solo trumpet plays the counter-melody in whole and half notes. This is a striking, musical effect. Notice that the two melodies are in the same octave and that they actually cross. This is satisfactory only because of the great contrast between the two parts. The ear is never confused, but readily recognizes the individuality of each part.

(f) A device often employed in writing counter-melodies is canonic imitation. Here the counter-melody is almost the same as the principal melody, but it is played an octave lower and a measure later.

(g) Occasionally, a well-known melody or a portion of one makes an effective counter-melody. In the finale of the MISSISSIPPI SUITE, it is thrilling to hear the trombones playing DIXIE while the other sections are playing their melodic parts.

FIGURATION

There are a number of kinds of figuration. Generally, figuration consists of short tones in a high register played somewhat rapidly. Sometimes a figuration is a variation on the theme. More frequently, figurations are variations based upon the harmony (rather than upon the melody), and they are likely to be rhythmic in character.

Ex. 237

ANDANTE
from "The Surprise Symphony"

J. Haydn
Arr. Merle J. Isaac

130

GYPSY LIFE
from "The Fortune Teller"

Victor Herbert
Arr. Merle J. Isaac

b. Andante
Fl., Cls.

pp
Vn.
p

RUMANIAN OVERTURE

Merle J. Isaac

c. Tempo di valse lento
Fl.
p
Hn.
mf

SANTA CLAUS IS COMIN' TO TOWN

Haven Gillespie, J. Fred Coots

d. Moderato
Fl., Cl.
mf
Vns.
mf

MISSISSIPPI SUITE
(Mardi Gras)

Ferde Grofe

e. Maestoso
Vns., Va.
ff
Tpts., Hns.
ff

GYPSY LIFE
from "The Fortune Teller"

Victor Herbert
Arr. Merle J. Isaac

f. Allegro
Xylo.
mf
Vn.
mf

Ex. 237 illustrates several characteristic passages.

(a) The figuration is largely a broken chord or arpeggio figure based upon the harmony of each measure. It is also a variation on the theme. Played by the violins, it is sometimes above and sometimes below the principal melody, played by the clarinet. This contrast in tone color permits the two parts to be in the same register and still be heard distinctly.

(b) The staccato woodwind rhythm-figures provide a charming accompaniment to the beautiful sustained violin melody.

(c) The horn has a sustained melody in the middle register, while the solo flute has a staccato figure in an upper register. There is contrast in tone color, register, rhythm, and style.

(d) In the first two measures, the figuration in the woodwinds is really a variation on the principal melody played by the violins. In the third and fourth measures, the woodwind figure is independent.

(e) This shows an effective form of figuration for violins and violas in a loud passage where the brass sustain. The figuration is essentially a rhythmic variation based on the harmonic background of the music.

(f) This brilliant figuration, played on the xylophone at a lively pace, is a variation on the principal melody. A large part of its effectiveness is due to the contrasting tone color and the staccato quality of the xylophone.

COMBINING THE PARTS

Among other things, orchestration is the art of combining melodies. In the foregoing pages we have discussed various combinations of two melodies: principal melody and bass melody, principal melody and counter-melody, and so on. In actual practice, several melodies must be combined so that they may be played simultaneously.

Ex. 238

LAURA

Johnny Mercer, David Raksin

Ex. 238 gives an excerpt from an arrangement of LAURA for string orchestra. The principal melody (c) is played by the cello in a tenor register. The bass part (d) is below, and the accompaniment parts (b) are both above and below the principal melody. Much higher, the violins (a) play melodic phrases, in thirds, which may be classified either as counter-melody or as figuration.

Since all of the string instruments have similar tone color, and the registers used here are quite close, an effective performance of this arrangement requires contrast in volume between the various parts.

The principal melody must be played the loudest so that it will be heard plainly. The bass part and the accompaniment parts should be played softly. The first violin part is most active when the cello part is sustaining and least active when the cello part is moving. This contrast in activity helps the ear to follow the two parts, possibly hearing them alternately.

Ex. 239

THE STARS AND STRIPES FOREVER

John Philip Sousa

Ex. 239 is an excerpt from the thrilling finale of THE STARS AND STRIPES FOREVER by John Philip Sousa. Study the various parts individually and in combinations. Observe how each part contributes to the ensemble.

DISSONANCE

When writing parts for the various orchestral instruments, check carefully for disagreeable or unintentional dissonances. For example, melodies A and B may sound well together, as do melodies A and C. But do not assume that melodies B and C will therefore sound well together. Check all parts against all other parts.

All dissonance is not disagreeable; some is desirable and even necessary. Seventh chords and suspensions are mildly dissonant and most effective, due largely to their resolutions.

A composer may write any dissonance he wishes. An arranger, too, may write dissonances, but he must write in keeping with the style of the composition. If the original number has conservative harmony, an unresolved dissonance added by the arranger might be entirely out of place.

No one, composer or arranger, should write dissonances unknowingly, carelessly, or inadvertently. Such dissonances are errors and oversights, indicating hurried and careless workmanship. They are not likely to be beautiful or effective.

Chapter Ten

BALANCE

The word *balance* refers to equitable distribution or relationship. As used in this chapter, balance refers to the degree of prominence given to each instrumental part in relation to the other parts.

The principal melody should always be prominent: other melodies must be less prominent. The accompaniment must be the least prominent. This aspect of balance (the horizontal) is discussed under the heading MELODIES.

The harmony must also be in balance. The chords in the accompaniment and those played by the full orchestra should have all of the tones played with suitable prominence. The root of the chord, the third, the fifth, and any other intervals should be in balance throughout the various registers and in the various instrumental families. This aspect of balance (the vertical) is discussed in the paragraphs dealing with CHORDS.

The arranger cannot be sure that his orchestration always will be played in proper balance, but he can write the parts in such a way that, when played reasonably well, the music will sound well balanced. To do this, he must be thoroughly acquainted with the capabilities and limitations of each of the orchestral instruments so that he can write playable, effective parts for them.

MELODIES

The principal melody must be prominent. It must be heard. It must be recognized immediately, without effort. The instruments playing the secondary melodies and the accompaniment must never overpower the principal melody in volume, brilliance, rhythm, or in any other way. This quality of prominence, essential to the principal melody, can be brought about in several ways:

1. By giving the melody to an instrument that is sure to be prominent: trumpet, oboe, etc. (Ex. 240 a, b);
2. By placing the melody in a higher octave where it will be prominent (Ex. 240 c);
3. By placing the melody at a distance from the accompaniment (Ex. 240 d);
4. By marking the proper relative degree of volume (*p, mf, f, etc.*) for each of the parts (Ex. 240 b, c, d). This device must not be used by a writer to correct errors in orchestration. For example, a flute passage in a low register marked *forte* is not likely to balance an oboe passage in a high register marked *piano*.

5. By giving the melody to two or more instruments, in unison or in octaves (Ex. 240 e, f, g, h). Doubling a melody gives it greater power. Doubling an octave higher adds brilliance and brightens the color. Doubling an octave lower adds solidity and darkens the color. However, doubling takes away some of the characteristic tone color and may alter the style and expression given the part by the players.

6. By placing the melody in the best register of the instrument playing it (Ex. 240 i). Wind instruments, especially, have one register in which they are at their best. Usually this is neither the highest register nor the lowest. On a string instrument (except the bass), a melody played on the top string usually achieves maximum prominence.

7. By writing the accompaniment in sufficiently different character so that it will permit the listener to hear the principal melody clearly (Ex. 240 j). This is especially necessary if the melody is in the middle register.

8. By writing the secondary melodies in such a way that the listener can distinguish them clearly and immediately recognize their functions. In Ex. 240 (k), two trumpets provide a rhythmic and harmonic background which differs greatly in character from the principal melody. The latter can be heard without effort as it is played by several instruments in unison and in octaves. Besides, the listener heard this melody earlier in the arrangement. Notice that the principal melody and the secondary melody alternate in activity: when one moves, the other sustains.

The preceding suggestions and the musical illustrations in Ex. 240 refer mainly to principal melodies. In general, the same *principles* apply to secondary melodies. We can make a secondary melody more or less prominent in several ways:

1. By the choice of instrument;
2. By the choice of register;
3. By the distance of the secondary melody from the principal melody;
4. By indicating dynamics in the parts;
5. By doubling or not doubling;
6. By writing secondary melodies different in character from the principal melody.

Balance, in this chapter, refers to the relative degree of prominence given to each of the parts.

Ex. 240

MELODIES

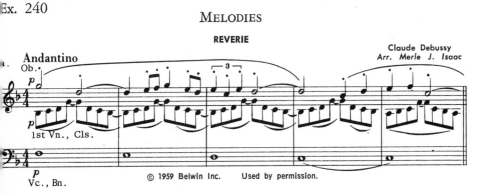

REVERIE

Claude Debussy
Arr. Merle J. Isaac

© 1959 Belwin Inc.   Used by permission.

VINCENT YOUMANS FANTASY
(More Than You Know)

William Rose, Edward Eliscu, Vincent Youmans

b. Moderate ballad tempo
Tpt. Solo (cup mute)

Vns., Va.

Vc., Db. © 1929, 1933 (Renewal 1957, 1961) Miller Music Corp. & Vincent Youmans Co. Inc.

SIBONEY

Ernesto Lecuona, Dolly Morse

c. Tempo di rhumba
1st Vn.

2nd Vn., Va.

Vc., Db. © 1929 (Renewal 1957) Leo Feist Inc.

GYPSY LIFE
from "The Fortune Teller"

Victor Herbert
Arr. Merle J. Isaac

d. Andante
1st Vn.

2nd Vn., Va.

Vc., Db. © 1955 Belwin Inc. Used by permission.

BALLET PARISIEN

Jacques Offenbach
Arr. Merle J. Isaac

e. Allegro moderato
1st Fl., 1st Cl., 1st Vn.

f. Tempo di valse
1st Fl.

1st Vn.

g. Tempo di valse
1st Vn.

Vc.

h. Tempo di valse
1st Vn.
2nd Vn.

Va., Vc.

© 1955 Carl Fischer Inc. Used by permission.

BALLET PARISIEN

Jacques Offenbach
Arr. Merle J. Isaac

RUMANIAN OVERTURE

Merle J. Isaac

TEMPTATION

Arthur Freed, Nacio Herb Brown

CHORDS

A chord consists of a root, third, fifth, seventh, and possibly other tones in this series. In an arrangement for orchestra, these various members of the chord should be in balance.

It is understood that the tone which is part of the principal melody is to be more prominent than any other part. In a chorale, the top part is likely to stand out because of its position, and usually the top part is the principal melody.

The suggestions which follow refer to chords, and stress the vertical aspects of music. They do not contradict the suggestions previously given concerning the horizontal aspects of music: the principal melody, the secondary melodies, and the accompaniment.

In simple harmony, consisting of triads, the root and third are more important than the fifth. In seventh chords, the fifth is frequently omitted or given to instruments that may not always be available (e.g., 3rd or 4th horn).

Some *rules* that apply to four-part harmony (such as, "Don't double the third") cannot always be applied to harmony of many parts (such as an orchestration). The *principles* of four-part harmony do apply, however, and must be observed.

VERTICAL SPACING

When arranging chords for orchestral instruments, the vertical spacing of the tones requires careful consideration. There are two important guiding principles:

1. *When writing four or more parts, keep them fairly equidistant* (except that the bass part may be at a greater distance from the other parts than they are from one another).

2. *Upper parts are usually spaced more closely than lower parts.* This principle is really a modification of the first.

Ex. 241

THE NATURAL HARMONIC SERIES

While not a chord in the usual sense, the natural harmonic series (Ex. 241) is often used as an example of good vertical spacing. Large intervals — octaves and fifths — are found between the lower harmonics in the series. Smaller intervals are found in the middle. Seconds occur between the highest harmonics.

The black notes in Ex. 241 represent natural harmonics that are out of tune according to our tempered scale.

STRING CHORDS

The members of the string family of instruments are more closely related to one another than are the members of the woodwind, brass, and percussion families.

String instruments have considerable uniformity of tone color, and they blend well with one another.

Although each string instrument has four strings differing from one another in color and in dynamics, the difference is slight compared with that found within the various registers of the wind instruments.

Well-spaced string parts, that are effective for each of the instruments, are likely to sound full and well balanced when played together.

Ex. 242

STRING CHORDS

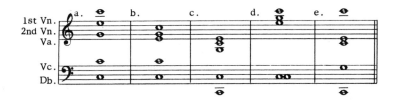

(a) Full and brilliant
(b) Full, though not brilliant
(c) Sonorous
(d) Thin; all top and bottom and no middle
(e) 1st Violin is too far from 2nd Violin and Viola (unless this is a violin solo with soft accompaniment)

WOODWIND CHORDS

Instruments of the woodwind family present additional, specific problems involving tone color and register.

These instruments differ widely in tone color and, when writing for the woodwind choir, the arranger must use great care in selecting tones that will blend.

The woodwind instruments have some registers in which it is difficult to play softly and other registers in which it is difficult to play loudly. Although skillful players can equalize them to some extent, these relatively strong and weak registers must be considered by the arranger.

Ex. 243

WOODWIND CHORDS

(a) Good
(b) Good
(c) Poor — Flute too soft, oboe too loud
(d) Poor — Flute not loud enough to balance clarinets
(e) Good — Harmony in open position
(f) Good — Harmony in close position

Notice that, in an orchestration, parts for the woodwind instruments are frequently written all top and bottom and no middle. This is because other instruments — string and brass — are sounding the chord tones in the middle register. The harmony in the woodwind section is complete, however, without the tones in the middle register.

BRASS CHORDS

The tone color of the brass instruments is more homogeneous than the tone color of the woodwinds, but less homogeneous than that of the strings.

The trumpet and trombone are quite similar in tone color.

The horn tone is normally more mellow and less penetrating than the tones of the trumpet and trombone.

The tuba blends well with all of the brasses.

Brass instruments have greater uniformity of register than the woodwind instruments, but less than the string instruments.

The trumpet, horn, and trombone can play softly or loudly throughout their various registers, except that their high tones tend to become loud and penetrating.

These instruments are less brilliant and less prominent in their middle and lower registers.

The tuba can be played softly or loudly in any register. It is most useful in the lower half of its compass.

Ex. 244

BRASS CHORDS

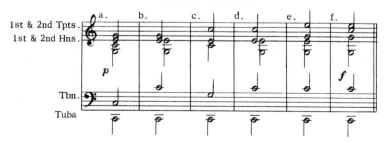

All of the arrangements in Ex. 244 are good. Some sound better played softly; others sound better played loudly.

In every case, the two trumpets are in thirds or sixths, and sound pleasing when played with or without the other instruments. Trumpet tones are very prominent, even when the full orchestra is playing, and trumpet parts should be written with this in mind.

When possible, two trumpets and a trombone should make complete harmony.

The horn parts, while not essential to the harmony, will add to the richness and fullness of the chord.

COMBINING THE FAMILIES

When playing chords, the harmony should be complete and in balance within each family of instruments. A chord played by the strings must contain the root, third, and fifth, or the harmony will sound incomplete. Similarly, the harmony must be complete and in balance within the woodwind section and within the brass section. For instance, the arranger may not give the root and fifth to the strings, and give the third to a woodwind instrument, expecting the harmony to sound complete.

When the harmony is complete within the strings, a wind part may be added which doubles the melody, in unison or in octaves. In this case, it is not necessary to have complete harmony in the wind section. It is only when playing harmony that a family must be complete within itself.

It is equally important that the families balance with one another and be equal in prominence, unless the difference is intentional. Assuming that the instruments are playing in similar registers, the families are fairly well balanced when the parts are played softly. In a loud passage, the brass choir dominates, both in volume and in color.

On string instruments, many short tones, played with separate bows, sound louder than long tones. On wind instruments, the opposite is true: a part consisting of long, sustained tones sounds louder than one consisting of tongued, short tones. (A possible exception to this might be a highly rhythmic passage for brass.)

Every instrument tends to lose its individual tone color when it plays just one short tone.

Generally speaking, the high tones on most instruments are the most prominent. This is not true of the bassoon, tuba, and some other bass instruments.

The high tones of bass instruments sound higher than tones of the same pitch in the low registers of treble instruments. For example, the note E on the first line of the treble staff sounds higher when played on a cello than when played on a violin.

Arrangers must guard against both: (a) all top and bottom and no middle; and (b) a heavy, muddy, middle register.

There are exceptions to all rules in music. The arranger must know and understand the rules in order to know when they may be set aside.

ORCHESTRA CHORDS

Ex. 245 shows, in condensed form, several chords arranged for the full orchestra. The first chord in each group shows the tones played by the string choir. The second chord shows the woodwind tones. The third, the brass. In the orchestration, all three groups are sounded together.

In general, the string tones are dispersed, the warmth and richness of the strings being distributed throughout the various registers.

Except for the bass clarinet and bassoon, the woodwind tones are mainly in the upper registers. The brass choir fills the middle and lower registers.

Each chord except (b) is the final chord of the composition indicated. The number of notes varies in the different arrangements because of different instrumentations.

Ex. 245

ORCHESTRA CHORDS

SOME PSYCHOLOGICAL FACTORS

For orchestral music to sound well balanced to the listener, the following psychological factors must be considered by the arranger:

1. The ear is likely to accept the highest part as the principal melody.
2. Listeners tend to follow a melodic and interesting part.
3. The ear is confused by overlapping parts, unless they are of contrasting tone color.
4. Players tend to bring out parts of melodic interest and importance.
5. A moving part attracts more attention than a sustained part (other things being equal).
6. Listeners are likely to recognize a theme of a composition when it is repeated, even though it is in a new setting and is less prominent.

SUMMARY

Balance, in orchestration, refers to the relative prominence of the parts, as melodies or as chord-tones.

Prominence depends on one or more of the following factors:

1. Instrumentation
2. Register
3. Tone color
4. Dynamics
5. Spacing
6. Rhythm
7. Style

Guides for vertical spacing:

1. Keep tones and parts fairly equidistant;
2. Upper parts are usually spaced more closely than lower parts.

String instruments are most homogeneous; brass instruments, next; woodwind instruments, least.

Various psychological factors merit consideration.

CHAPTER ELEVEN

WRITING THE SCORE

The first step in making an orchestration consists of selecting the composition to be orchestrated. This may be one of your own compositions, a number written by someone else, or it may be folk music. It may be already arranged for piano, voices, band, or some other combination of instruments. *If it is a copyrighted work, it is necessary to secure permission from the copyright owner before making any arrangement of it, for profit or not!*

THE SKETCH

Ex. 246
WORK SHEET

TITLE OF COMPOSITION

Composer ....

Arranger ....

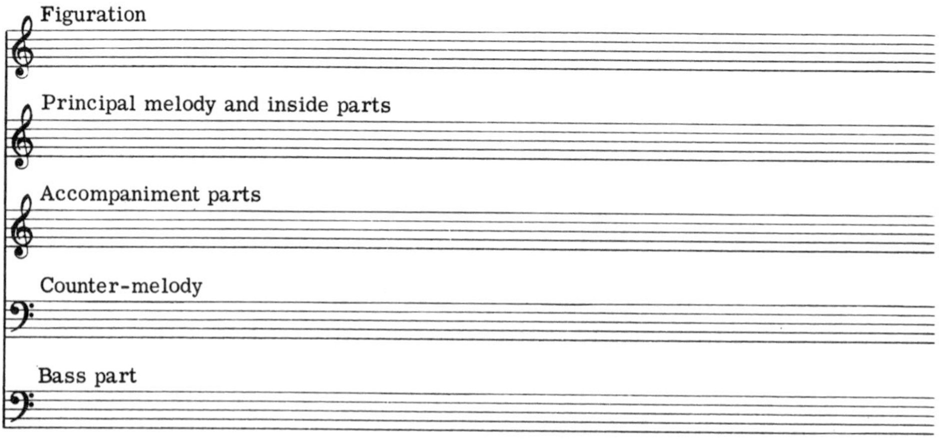

Figuration

Principal melody and inside parts

Accompaniment parts

Counter-melody

Bass part

The second step consists in making a sketch of the selected music, using a work sheet (with three to five staves) as illustrated in Ex. 246. This preliminary sketch on the work sheet is most important. It should be fully and completely written out, showing all melodies and harmonies. In working it out, the following questions must be considered and answered (tentatively, at least):

1. What will the completed arrangement be suitable for — concert, contest, theater, ballet, instruction?

2. What grade of difficulty will the arrangement be — difficult, medium, easy?

3. What will be the most effective key? (If the key of the arrangement is to be different from the key of the composition in its original form, the sketch — on the work sheet — will take care of much of the transposition and help to prevent errors.)

4. Which instruments are to carry the principal melody in the various sections of the piece? In which octaves?

5. Is the bass line satisfactory in its original form? Must it be re-written to make it more melodic, more interesting, more playable?

6. Is the harmony satisfactory in the original? (It is best not to change the principal melody, the bass line, or the harmony unless the changes are definite improvements.)

7. What kind of accompaniment: sustained or rhythmic? Which instruments will play the accompaniment?

8. What about counter-melodies? Will they be above or below the principal melodies? Which instruments will play them?

9. What about figuration? Where and who?

10. Will there be any special effects: solos, muted or pizzicato strings, muted brass, or percussion effects?

11. Will it be necessary to write an introduction, interlude, modulation, or coda?

12. What about tempos, including ritardandos and accelerandos?

13. What about dynamics and other marks of expression?

THE COMPLETED SKETCH

When the preliminary sketch is completely written out and checked at the piano (Ex. 247), it will give the arranger the following information and material to work with:

1. Suggestions regarding style.
2. Suggestions concerning grade of difficulty.
3. The key or keys of the selection.
4. The principal melodies and suggestions as to which instruments will play them.
5. The bass line.
6. The harmony.
7. The nature of the accompaniment and which instruments will provide it.
8. The counter-melodies and who are to play them.
9. The figuration, with designated instruments.

146

10. Definite suggestions as to special effects.
11. Tempos.
12. Marks of expression.

In addition, the sketch should show the rehearsal numbers (in red), an every measure should be numbered (in blue).

Ex. 247
WORK SHEET

THROUGH THE YEARS

Edward Heyman, Vincent Youman
Arr. Merle J. Isaac

© 1931 (Renewal 1959) Miller Music Corp. & Vincent Youmans Co. Inc.

THE MANUSCRIPT PAPER

After the sketch is completed and thoroughly checked, it is time to pr pare the manuscript paper for the full score. The paper should contain fro 12 to 24 staves, depending on the number of instrumental parts to be writte (It is customary to write two parts on one staff for some of the wind instr ments, especially those having fewer notes.)

Score paper with the names of the instruments (and clefs) printed the left end of each line is available. Although the printed instrumentatic is seldom exactly what is needed, it is easy to make a few changes in t printed names of the instruments.

THE LAYOUT

The arranger will find that his work will be easier, later on, if he carefully plans the layout of the score. Count the total number of measures in the composition, as shown in the sketch. Determine the approximate number of pages needed for the score.

Plan to put from four to six measures on a page if the measures are moderately long (contain many notes). Put from six to eight measures on a page if they are quite short (contain few notes).

The size of a measure in the score is determined by the number of notes in the part which has the most notes. Check the violin, flute, and clarinet parts, as these instruments usually have the largest number of notes to play. When checking, remember that accidentals take up as much room as notes in the staff, horizontally, and that notes on leger lines require more room than notes on the staff. DO NOT CROWD THE SCORE. Allow several extra pages.

Having determined the number of pages needed, take the necessary number of sheets of manuscript paper (there are four pages on each sheet), gather them together in book form, and number the pages.

PAGE ONE

On page one, the front cover, type or print very neatly the title of the composition, the composer's name, the arranger's name, the date, and other pertinent information. The music will then begin on page two, the inside front cover.

PAGE TWO

Page two requires the following preparations:

1. Write the names of the instruments in the left margin (unless they are already printed there).

2. Draw a vertical line from top to bottom at the extreme left end of the staves. (This line shows that all of the staves on the page are to be read together as a score, not consecutively as in a part.)

3. Add braces to indicate the grouping of the staves according to the families of instruments: woodwind, brass, percussion, and string. Later, the bar-lines also will group the staves into families of instruments. (This grouping makes score writing and score reading easier.)

4. Put in the proper clef for each instrument, and the key-signature. However, before we can write in the key-signature we must decide whether to write a C score or a transposed score.

THROUGH THE YEARS

Edward Heyman, Vincent Youmans

Ex. 248a
C Score

Andante con tristezza (*pensively*)

149

THROUGH THE YEARS

Edward Heyman, Vincent Youmans

Ex. 248b

Transposed Score Andante con tristezza (*pensively*)

Cantabile (♩=132)

Andante con tristezza (*pensively*)

1 Cantabile (♩=132)

THE C SCORE

A C score, shown in Ex. 248(a), is one that shows the *tones* played on each instrument as they actually sound (except for octave transpositions). A transposed score, Ex. 248(b), is one that shows the *notes* exactly as they are written in the parts. If this is not clear, refer to the chapter on transposition (page 93).

Students of orchestration, faced with a multitude of new problems, will be less likely to make mistakes writing a C score.

The various parts, separately or together, can be played on the piano without transposing any of them.

The accuracy of the notes and the completeness of the harmony can thus be checked more easily.

The arranger writing a C score must be especially careful to keep the parts within the playing range of the various transposing instruments (particularly the horns and saxophones).

Later, when the parts are extracted from the score, the necessary transpositions can be made with little difficulty. The copyist, with no problems of harmony or orchestration to think about, can concentrate on the transposition.

THE TRANSPOSED SCORE

The transposed score, shown in Ex. 248(b), is the traditional professional score. Almost all published scores are transposed scores. A conductor can read these scores without difficulty, even though they are not easy to play on the piano. The arranger writing a transposed score is less likely to write parts that are too high or too low.

THE SIGNATURES

After deciding whether to write a C score or a transposed score, the correct key-signatures and the time-signatures should be placed at the beginning of each line on page two, immediately after the clefs. *Do not crowd them.*

Refer to your sketch, and decide how many measures to have on page two. Remember that it is better to put only four measures on a page and have too much room, than to put eight measures on a page and not have enough room.

Unless there is a great deal of difference between the various measures, it is simpler to make them the same size.

THE BAR-LINES

With a ruler or dividers, divide the bottom line of the page into the desired number of measures. (Allow extra room in the first measure for the signatures.)

Using a T-square, draw the vertical bar-lines, stopping between the various families of instruments. Use a continuous bar-line for the woodwinds, another for the brass, and so on.

If you do not use a T-square, divide the top line as well as the bottom line, and draw the bar-lines using a ruler.

THE GUIDE LINES

Unless the measures are short, it will be found helpful to draw a light, vertical guide line in the center of each measure (possibly with a blue pencil). These guide lines will help in aligning the notes which are to be sounded together, a very important matter in score writing (and reading).

PREPARING THE PAGES

Keeping an eye on the sketch, the arranger may go ahead with the next few pages:

1. Write the names of the instruments in the left margin of each page (unless they are already printed there). The names may be abbreviated as shown in the chapter on notation (page 92).

2. Draw the score-line and braces at the left end of the staves.

3. Write the clefs and key-signatures for all of the instruments on each page.

4. Remember that the time-signature is given only once: at the beginning. However, each change of time (or meter) must be indicated.

5. Draw the bar-lines and the guide lines.

6. Number each measure at the top of the page, using blue pencil. This will help prevent the error of omitting measures.

7. Rehearsal numbers, circled in red, should be placed at the top and bottom of the page, preferably over bar-lines.

PUTTING MUSIC IN THE SCORE

Going back to page 2 of the score, the student may now start putting music in the full score. First, write in the principal melody. Second, write the bass. Then, write whatever seems natural. Follow the sketch closely. Check your work constantly. Have a soft pencil eraser handy, and do not hesitate to use it.

If you decide to write something in the score that is different from the way it is written in the sketch, be sure to change the sketch. A change in the part for one instrument is likely to require a change in other parts. Write down each change as you make it, both in the sketch and in the score. Do not depend upon your memory.

NEATNESS AND ACCURACY

Be neat! Write legibly. Space the notes and rests accurately. Watch the vertical alignment. Notes that are sounded together must be written exactly above and below one another. The same principle applies to rests.

Mistakes in the full score may be copied into the parts and cause severe trouble at the first rehearsal. If there are many errors in the manuscript, the conductor and the players will lose interest in the music. Either they will not play it well, or they may decide not to play it at all!

BE NEAT! BE ACCURATE!

EXTENDED RESTS

Notation must be as clear and definite as possible. All measures should be filled completely with notes or rests. Whole-rests should be placed and centered in all measures of the score where there are no notes. Blank measures suggest that the arrangement is unfinished.

In most orchestrations there are times when certain instruments are not playing. The entire brass section may have a sixteen-measure rest during a quiet passage. Professional scores (and miniature scores) often omit the staves for the instruments which are not playing for a page or two. This may make it possible to have two scores on a page, reducing the total number of pages in the score.

This procedure is not recommended for student arrangers. It saves paper, but it makes score writing and score reading more difficult. (Besides, the arranger may decide later on to add muted brass during that quiet passage.)

ABBREVIATIONS

Professional arrangers make use of many abbreviations in their manuscript scores and parts. Abbreviations present incomplete pictures, and less experienced arrangers should not use them (thereby avoiding possible errors). Refer to this subject in the chapter on notation (page 91).

DIRECTIONS

Directions which apply to the entire orchestra, such as tempo and mood (e.g., *Allegro con spirito*), may be indicated at the top of the page and near the bottom (above the first violin line).

Marks which indicate expression, dynamics, and style must be included in each part.

When only one part is written on a staff in the score that is being used for two wind instruments, indicate whether the part is for the 1st or 2nd instrument, or for both (*a*2).

Remember that most directions in music are to be followed until they are cancelled or changed in some way. For example, if a passage in a string part is marked *pizzicato*, the players must continue to play their notes in this manner until the direction *arco* appears. This rule applies to directions such as the following: muted, *ritardando, accelerando, solo, crescendo,* and *decrescendo.*

PENCIL OR INK?

The original full score, written by a student or a non-professional arranger, should be written in pencil so that changes and corrections may be made when needed. A full score that is intended for professional use should be written in ink.

CHECKING

When the full score is completed, it must be checked and re-checked before the parts are extracted. It is well to check the last measure on each right-hand page with the first measure on the following left-hand page. Unless a double-bar separates them, they should form a melodic sequence. Play the various parts separately and in combinations — slowly, critically, and patiently.

Try to find ways of improving the melodic quality of each part and the harmonic sonority of the combined parts. Never be quite satisfied.

Seek ways to polish and refine each melodic phrase, each harmonic progression. In the art of music, there is no room for error or crudity. A musical masterpiece is faultless and beautiful.

CHAPTER TWELVE

EXTRACTING THE PARTS

There are many steps and stages between the musical idea in the composer's mind and the musical tones heard by an audience in a concert hall. Some of the steps are more interesting, even more exciting, than others, but all are important, all are essential.

One step in the process of making music is that of copying the parts for the players from the full score. While this may seem to be largely labor, it requires knowledge, skill, and alertness.

The first step in extracting the parts consists of studying the score carefully. Look for errors and omissions. Be sure that the score is complete and correct in every detail.

Check for tempo indications (including *rit., accel.,* and *a tempo*).

See that all expression marks have been placed where needed.

Add the bowings for the string instruments. It may be found more convenient to mark the bowings in the extracted parts first, and then add them to the full score.

Check for wind instrument articulation markings.

The score should show where cue notes are to be included in the parts.

The score should have rehearsal numbers, and every measure should be numbered.

Note the length of the arrangement, and plan the layout of the parts. Can a part be written on one page without crowding? Or will it require two, three, or more pages?

For most orchestra parts, 12-line paper is satisfactory. However, 10-line paper which has more room between the staves should be used if there are many leger lines, fingerings, or other markings above or below the staff.

The parts are always written in ink, *black* ink. For greater clarity and contrast, the cue notes found in the parts may be written in red ink.

All notation should enable the eye to read quickly, easily, and accurately. Do not crowd your manuscript!

Notes, rests, and all other symbols must be large enough to be read easily from a distance. Remember that some of the players sit or stand quite a distance from their music.

Plan for page turning. A player needs a little time to turn a page. He can do this best when he has a few measures rest. If the part fills just two pages, write it on the same side of a double sheet of manuscript paper so that it can be played without any page-turning.

Write separate parts for each instrument. Never put two parts on one sheet (and on one staff) unless they are almost entirely in unison.

Every piece of manuscript must be well identified. At the top of the first page of an orchestra part, the following information should appear:

1. The name of the instrument for which the part has been written.
2. The title of the composition.
3. The composer's name.
4. The arranger's name or initials.

At the top of the second page, and any other pages that follow, the name of the instrument and the page number should be indicated.

Write key-signatures for all instruments except those members of the percussion family that do not have definite pitch. Use key-signatures in the parts for the horns, timpani, and bells.

Check list: after the first word, you usually need the second:

rit. — *a tempo*
accel. — *a tempo*
pizz. — *arco*
muted — open

Rehearsal numbers should be placed over the bar-lines whenever possible, and they should be conspicuous. The numbers may be enclosed with squares or circles. They may be black or red, but they must be easily and quickly found. After a part is extracted, check over the rehearsal numbers for omissions.

When extracting parts from a full score, the copyist may start at the top of the first page and copy out the entire part for the first flute. Then, he may take the part for the second flute, and so on with all the other instruments in the order in which they appear on the page.

Another method is to copy all of the C parts, then all of the parts in Bb, Eb, and F — thus grouping the parts having the same transposition. In this way, the transposition becomes more of a habit and less of a hazard. (This method is more applicable to the C score than to the transposed score.)

Most copyists include the various markings in the music as they write the notes. Another method is to copy all of the notes for all of the parts — and then go back and put in the marks of expression, etc. With this procedure, there is likely to be more uniformity in the parts and fewer omissions of markings.

These markings are essential. Every page must have, in addition to the notes, directions on how to play the notes. The part must indicate tempo and tempo changes, expression and dynamics, style and bowings or articulations, when to put mutes on and when to take them off, and any other directions necessary to secure satisfactory performance. Indicate the exact point at which a *crescendo* or a *diminuendo* begins and ends. This should usually be the same in all parts.

The copyist must check and re-check his work. Parts must not contain wrong notes nor omit accidentals, key changes, and other vital information. Mistakes must be found and corrected before the music is given to the players. Sour notes at the first rehearsal should never be the fault of the arranger or the copyist!

A complete set of parts of an orchestration includes one part for each of the wind instruments. That is, there is a part for the first flute and one for the second flute. There may be two or four flute players in the orchestra, but one copy of each part is standard procedure.

The percussion section will need one part for the timpani, one for the drums, etc., and possibly one for the mallet percussives. A bell part, if it is short, may be included in either the timpani part or the drum part if one of them has rests at that time and is free to double. A prominent bell part may require a separate sheet of music.

With the string parts, there is an added problem. Several copies of each string part are included in a set of parts. This might be 8-8-5-5-5 (8 copies of the first violin part, 8 of the 2nd violin part, 5 viola, 5 cello, and 5 bass parts). If parts have been written for advanced violin and/or third violin, it is well to have more than one copy of each.

Whenever two or more copies of any manuscript part are needed, the copyist may consider the various processes available for duplicating manuscript by photographic means. While this incurs some expense, it saves a great deal of time, and the parts so duplicated will be exactly the same.

At this point it may be well to remind the copyist that it is illegal to duplicate any copyrighted music by photographic processes or by any other means — for profit or not — without first securing permission from the copyright owner.

"Ignorance of the law excuses no man." Every arranger, copyist, and student should know the fundamentals of the federal copyright law. It will be found helpful to study Chapter 14.

CHAPTER THIRTEEN

PIANO-CONDUCTOR PARTS

Published compositions and arrangements for orchestra, other than symphonic music, usually include a part that is marked *Piano-Conductor*. This part serves a dual purpose: it gives the notes to be played by the pianist (if there is one), and it provides notes to be read by the conductor.

At one time, piano parts were merely accompaniment parts written on two staves, with the principal melody written above in small notes (Ex. 249a). Since a piano accompaniment part may be somewhat monotonous, the cued-in melody line helped the pianist to keep his place in the music.

Later, the principal melody was written on a third staff placed above the two staves of the actual piano part (Ex. 249b).

Gradually more parts were cued in. Wind parts were added above the pianist's treble staff. Cello and trombone parts were cued in the bass clef staff (Ex. 249c).

Ex. 249

THE BAND PLAYED ON

Waitz from the Ballet Suite
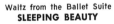

BALLET PARISIEN

C.

Tempo di valse

Jacques Offenbach
Arr. Merle J. Isaac

© 1955 Carl Fischer Inc.   Used by permission.

With a good professional orchestra, a conductor can achieve a successful performance using a condensed score similar to the one shown in Ex. 249(c). The conductor may not know what each instrument is supposed to play, but he will be aware of the more important melodies, the harmony, and some of the special effects (such as a cymbal crash).

With an amateur orchestra, a conductor needs more information. Less skillful players require help in interpreting the notes written in their parts. If the conductor is to give assistance to these players, he should know what their notes are.

A full score is the best score — especially with non-professional players. Full scores, however, are expensive to print, and most publishers substitute a condensed piano-conductor part for the full score.

Ex. 250 shows a three-line piano-conductor part. An experienced conductor can tell what notes are to be played by the string instruments, but he cannot be sure about the wind and percussion instruments.

The four-line piano-conductor part shown in Ex. 251 gives much more information for the conductor. All of the string parts are shown, as well as some of the wind and percussion parts. Notice that, as the part contains more information for the conductor, it becomes increasingly difficult for the pianist to find and read his part.

As the orchestration becomes more intricate, additional lines are needed in the conductor part. Examples 252(a) and 252(b) show a five-line piano conductor part. In general, the plan is as follows:

1st line — Violins and Viola
2nd line — Woodwind instruments
3rd line — Brass instruments
4th and 5th lines — Piano part
5th line — Cello and Bass

This plan is not fixed: it can be varied to meet the needs of the passage. Percussion parts can be shown if desired.

In Example 252(a), the five lines are not essential in the opening strain of the composition. Later, as shown in Example 252(b), the parts are more active and more independent, and having five lines is a distinct advantage.

Ex. 250

ALICE BLUE GOWN

Joseph McCarthy, Harry Tierney

162

Ex. 251

OVER THE RAINBOW

E. Y. Harburg, Harold Arlen

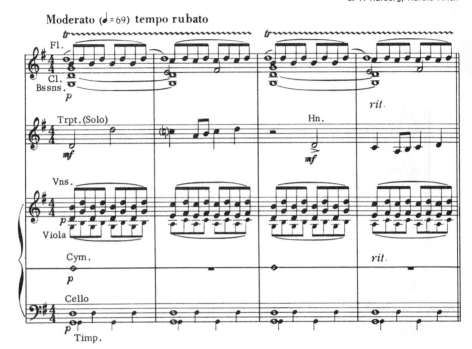

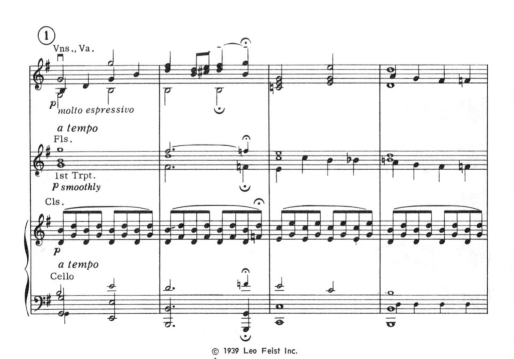

Ex. 252a

SERENATA D'AMORE

Mantovani

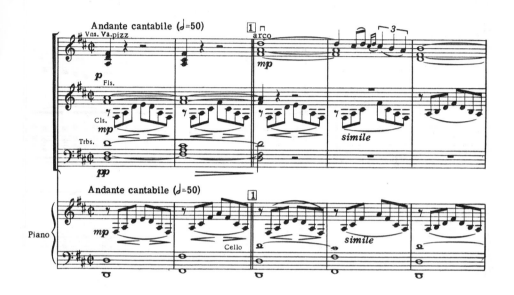

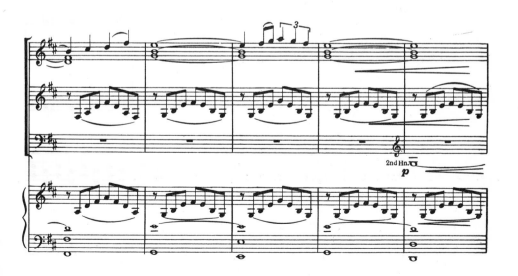

Ex. 252b

SERENATA D'AMORE

Mantovani

Piano-conductor parts, while practical and economical, are never entirely satisfactory. Limitations of space necessitate the omission of many important parts. The trend is toward conductor parts having more lines.

With some types of music (fairly simple, with limited instrumentation), the 8-line score is adequate (Ex. 253). This score may have lines for the following groups of instruments:

Line 1—Flute, Oboe	Line 5—Trombone, Tuba
" 2—Bb Clarinets	" 6—Drums
" 3—Bb Trumpets	" 7—Violins, Viola
" 4—F Horns	" 8—Cello, Bass

With the 8-line score, a separate piano-accompaniment part is needed.

Ex. 253

WIN, TEAM, WIN
(March)

Merle J. Isaac

166

A piano part may be a rhythmic, harmonic accompaniment part (Ex. 254a, b, c, d, e) or it may be more pianistic (Ex. 254f, g, h).

In any case, the piano part (as any other part) must be well written. One must know what is practical and effective on the instrument. Some chords and chord sequences are quite playable, while others are awkward and difficult. To write well for the piano, it is most helpful to be able to play the piano.

One who studies well-written piano parts will find many concrete examples of effective piano idioms.

Ex. 254

a.

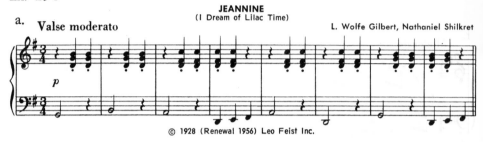

JEANNINE
(I Dream of Lilac Time)
L. Wolfe Gilbert, Nathaniel Shilkret

Valse moderato

© 1928 (Renewal 1956) Leo Feist Inc.

b.

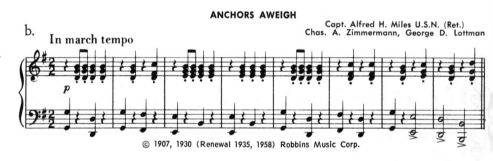

ANCHORS AWEIGH
Capt. Alfred H. Miles U.S.N. (Ret.)
Chas. A. Zimmermann, George D. Lottman

In march tempo

© 1907, 1930 (Renewal 1935, 1958) Robbins Music Corp.

c.

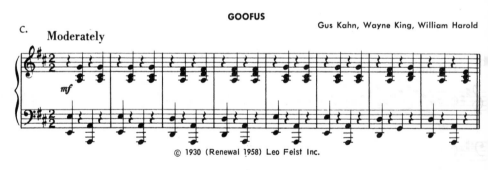

GOOFUS
Gus Kahn, Wayne King, William Harold

Moderately

© 1930 (Renewal 1958) Leo Feist Inc.

d.

OYE NEGRA
(Guaracha)
Noro Morales

Tempo di guaracha

© 1942 Robbins Music Corp.

TEMPTATION

Arthur Freed, Nacio Herb Brown

e. Moderate beguine tempo

OVER THE RAINBOW

E. Y. Harburg, Harold Arlen

f. Moderato

SANTA CLAUS IS COMIN' TO TOWN

Haven Gillespie, J. Fred Coots

g. Moderato

SERENATA D'AMORE

Mantovani

h. Andante cantabile

CHAPTER FOURTEEN

AN ARRANGER MUST KNOW ABOUT COPYRIGHT

"What music am I, as an arranger, free to use?"

"Am I free to make copies of my arrangement of published works for use by a school orchestra?"

"Am I free to allow an orchestra to give public performance of my arrangement of a published work?"

These are only a few of the questions an arranger must answer before he begins to make an arrangement of a published composition. To answer them, an arranger must know about the Copyright Law.

The Copyright Law provides protection in the following three broad classifications of creative endeavor in the musical field:

1. DRAMATIC-MUSICAL WORKS: operas, operettas, musical comedies, and similar works.
2. MUSICAL COMPOSITIONS: vocal and instrumental compositions.
3. BOOKS: librettos, poems, and lyrics without music.

There is one thing an arranger must do if the music he intends to arrange is copyrighted: HE MUST OBTAIN THE PERMISSION OF THE COPYRIGHT OWNER. Arranging a musical composition without the permission of the copyright owner is an infringement of copyright.

The copyright notice is always on the title page of a published work or on the back of the title page. On sheet music and parts of orchestrations, the copyright notice is at the bottom of the first page of the music. The notice includes the word "Copyright" and the symbol ©, the year in which the music was copyrighted, and the name of the copyright owner. An address, also, is usually given.

If you wish to make an arrangement of a copyrighted work, you must write for permission. If the copyright is owned by an individual, write to him in care of the publisher, who will forward your request. If the copyright is owned by a publisher, write to that publisher.

Tell the copyright owner the exact title and date of the composition you wish to arrange. Tell him exactly what purpose you wish to make of his work:

1. as an exercise in arranging;
2. for school band or orchestra rehearsals;
3. for public performance — when, where, by whom;
4. what instrumentation will be used;
5. whether or not a donation or admission fee will be charged for the performance;
6. how you plan to reproduce copies, and how many.

Copyright owners are free to request not only a finished copy of your arrangement (after they have given permission for its use), but also a fee for each copy made. They also have the right, however, to give permission without demanding a fee.

In the case of materials published outside the United States, the laws require no specific notice of copyright, and inquiry as to copyright status should therefore be made of the publisher or his American representative.

There are some educators who have the mistaken impression that copying and reproducing copyrighted material is permissible and legal as long as the copied material is not sold for profit. *This is not so,* and publishers take a dim view of such procedures. Composers and publishers invest much time, talent, and capital in their work. They are entitled to income and profit from the use of their published works.

Reproducing published music, by any process, is an unfair practice because it deprives the composer and his publisher of just royalties and sales. What is even more serious, this practice is a violation of the Copyright Law, and severe penalties have been provided.

The following are phrases taken from the Copyright Law:

"Any person entitled thereto (the person securing the copyright) ... *shall have the exclusive right*

1. to print, reprint, publish, copy, and vend the copyrighted work;
2. to arrange or adapt it, if it be a musical work;
3. to perform the copyrighted work publicly for profit, if it be a musical composition;
4. to make any arrangement or setting of it, or of the melody of it, in any system of notation."

"Any person who willfully and for profit shall infringe any copyright secured by this title, or who shall knowingly and willfully aid or abet such infringement, shall be deemed guilty of a misdemeanor, and upon conviction thereof shall be punished by imprisonment for not exceeding one year or by a fine of not less than one hundred dollars nor more than one thousand dollars, or both, in the discretion of the court."

The law is specific and clear. *In spirit and in fact you are guilty of infringement if you through act or sanction, without express permission of the copyright owner, do any of the following:*

1. Make any arrangement of copyrighted music;
2. Copy or reproduce extra parts for your band or orchestra;
3. Make a songslide of a copyrighted song;
4. Reproduce copyrighted words or music through the use of the mimeograph, multilith, photostat, ozalid process, *or any other process.*

Legally, therefore, one may arrange music that falls into the following categories:

1. Compositions in the public domain (PD):
   a. Folksongs;
   b. Compositions for which the copyright has expired. (In countries other than the United States, the copyright extends to 50 years after the death of the composer.)
2. Copyrighted compositions for which permission to make a specific arrangement has been granted by the copyright owner;
3. Original compositions of the arranger.

In recent years, machines capable of reproducing manuscript music have appeared on the market. These devices are a boon to the arranger and copyist who may need several copies of certain parts. It is permissible to use these reproducing machines *only* if the music reproduced falls in any of the above categories.

It is interesting to note that an arranger in the course of his work also fulfills the function of a composer. Utilizing harmony, counterpoint, form, rhythm, and composition, the arranger may take a musical idea and create a completely new setting for it. The arranger is limited in what he may create only by his originality and technique. However, he must always obtain the permission of the copyright owner.

In order to be acceptable for copyright registration, an idea, in music, must be a completely developed melody. The length is immaterial. Even a two-measure melody, complete within itself, may be registered.

Before a composer can legally claim a musical idea as his own, he must first put the idea in tangible, visible form. To accomplish this, the music must appear in music notation on paper. The present Copyright Law does not grant protection to a musical idea recorded on a disk or on tape. One cannot look at the grooves in a disk or at a tape and visually determine the musical idea.

It is easy to obtain copyright in the United States. If a new original work is unpublished, the composer may fill out the proper form (secured by writing the Register of Copyrights) and send it, together with the specified fee and a copy of the composition, to the Register of Copyrights, Washington, D. C. After the composition has been filed in the Copyright Office, the composer will receive a Certificate of Copyright.

If a new composition is published, copyright is obtained by the mere act of publication (i.e., offering copies for sale to the public) with the proper notice of copyright. In addition, the law provides for registration which takes place after publication. To accomplish this step the publisher must send two printed copies (with notice of copyright), together with the specified form and fee, to the Register of Copyrights. An International Copyright also may be secured according to the rules and regulations of the Berne Copyright Convention, the Brussels revision, and the Universal Copyright Convention.

In the United States, the copyright of a musical composition extends over a period of 28 years following the registration of an unpublished work or the publication of a work offered for sale. During the last year of this 28 year period of copyright, a renewal term of an additional 28 years is available to the author, if living; otherwise, to those in interest through him. At the end of this time, 56 years*, the composition is said to be in the public domain (PD).

It is possible to copyright a new arrangement of a composition in the public domain by creating an adaptation which has sufficient originality and new material to merit a copyright of its own.

A thorough understanding of the material in this chapter is, therefore, of great importance to the arranger. Application of this knowledge helps the arranger to avoid the hazards of infringement; aids him to recognize compositions in the public domain and those that are copyrighted; teaches him to obtain permission when planning an arrangement of a copyrighted work; and warns him against reproducing copyrighted music or words by any photographic or other duplicating process. Above all, this knowledge should engender a healthy respect for copyright and thus enable the arranger to create freely with full awareness of the law.

*At the time this book is going to print, certain important changes have been proposed by the Register of Copyrights based upon suggestions of copyright experts, as a basis for Congressional action toward a major revision in the Copyright Law. One of these suggestions is to increase the length of the copyright to one term of 76 years.

BIBLIOGRAPHY

Donato, Anthony, *Preparing Music Manuscript,* Prentice-Hall, Inc., Englewood Cliffs, N. J., 1963.

Downey, Lyle and Johnson, Harold, *Basic Orchestration Workbook,* Wm. C. Brown Co., Dubuque, Iowa, 1953.

Dunn, John P., *A Student's Guide to Orchestration,* Novello and Co., London, 1928.

Forsyth, Cecil, *Orchestration,* Macmillan Co., New York, 1935.

Gehrkens, Karl W., *Music Notation and Terminology,* Laidlaw Bros., Chicago, 1930.

Goetschius, Percy, *Exercises in Melody Writing,* G. Schirmer, Inc., New York, 1928.

Harris, Clement A., *How to Write Music,* H. W. Gray Co., New York, 1917.

Heacox, Arthur E., *Project Lessons in Orchestration,* Oliver Ditson Co., Philadelphia, 1928.

Hendrickson, Clarence V., *Instrumentalists' Handy Reference Manual,* Carl Fischer, Inc., New York, 1957.

Isaac, Merle J. and Levin, Joseph A., *Instrumentally Yours,* Robbins Music Corporation, New York, 1958.

Jacob, Archibald, *Musical Handwriting,* Oxford University Press, London, 1947.

Johnson, Harold M., *How to Write Music Manuscript,* Carl Fischer, Inc., New York, 1946.

Kennan, Kent Wheeler, *The Technique of Orchestration,* Prentice-Hall, Inc., Englewood Cliffs, N. J., 1952.

Leibowitz, René and Maguire, Jan, *Thinking for Orchestra,* G. Schirmer, Inc., New York, 1960.

McKay, George Frederick, *Creative Orchestration,* Allyn and Bacon, Inc., Boston, 1963.

Miller, Roy M., *Practical Instrumentation for the Wind Band,* Wm. C. Brown Co., Dubuque, Iowa, 1948.

Piston, Walter, *Orchestration,* W. W. Norton & Co., Inc., New York, 1955.

Rimsky-Korsakov, N., *Principles of Orchestration,* 3rd ed., Edwin F. Kalmus, Inc., New York, 1938.

Rogers, Bernard, *The Art of Orchestration,* Appleton-Century-Crofts, Inc., New York, 1951.

Tapper, Thomas, *First Year Melody Writing,* Arthur P. Schmidt Co., New York, 1938.

Wagner, Joseph, *Orchestration,* McGraw-Hill Book Co., Inc., New York, 1959.

Wilson, Harry Robert, *Choral Arranging for Schools, Glee Clubs, and Publication,* Robbins Music Corporation, New York, 1949.

Yoder, Paul, *Arranging Method for School Bands,* Robbins Music Corporation, New York, 1946.